lonely planet

Pocket
LOS ANGELES

TOP SIGHTS • LOCAL LIFE • MADE EASY

Andrew Bender, Cristian Bonetto

In This Book

QuickStart Guide

Your keys to understanding the city – we help you decide what to do and how to do it

Need to Know
Tips for a smooth trip

Neighborhoods
What's where

Explore Los Angeles

The best things to see and do, neighborhood by neighborhood

Top Sights
Make the most of your visit

Local Life
The insider's city

The Best of Los Angeles

The city's highlights in handy lists to help you plan

Best Walks
See the city on foot

Los Angeles' Best...
The best experiences

Survival Guide

Tips and tricks for a seamless, hassle-free city experience

Getting Around
Travel like a local

Essential Information
Including where to stay

Our selection of the city's best places to eat, drink and experience:

⊙ Sights

⊗ Eating

⊖ Drinking

✪ Entertainment

⊕ Shopping

These symbols give you the vital information for each listing:

☏ Telephone Numbers	✦ Family-Friendly
☉ Opening Hours	✿ Pet-Friendly
P Parking	☐ Bus
Nonsmoking	☐ Ferry
@ Internet Access	M Metro
☎ Wi-Fi Access	S Subway
✈ Vegetarian Selection	☐ Tram
☐ English-Language Menu	☐ Train

Find each listing quickly on maps for each neighborhood:

Bar Hemingway

16 ⊖ Map p233, B2

Legend has it that Hemi self, wielding a machine rate this timber-pan ered bar during showpiece is a n by Papa ar town. Dress s.com; Hôtel Rit ☉6.30pm-2a

Lonely Planet's
Los Angeles

Lonely Planet Pocket Guides are designed to get you straight to the heart of the city.

Inside you'll find all the must-see sights, plus tips to make your visit to each one really memorable. We've split the city into easy-to-navigate neighborhoods and provided clear maps so you'll find your way around with ease. Our expert authors have searched out the best of the city: walks, food, nightlife and shopping, to name a few. Because you want to explore, our 'Local Life' pages will take you to some of the most exciting areas to experience the real Los Angeles.

And of course you'll find all the practical tips you need for a smooth trip: itineraries for short visits, how to get around, and how much to tip the guy who serves you a drink at the end of a long day's exploration.

It's your guarantee of a really great experience.

Our Promise

You can trust our travel information because Lonely Planet authors visit the places we write about, each and every edition. We never accept freebies for positive coverage, so you can rely on us to tell it like it is.

QuickStart Guide **7**

Explore Los Angeles **21**

Worth a Trip:

QuickStart Guide

Welcome to Los Angeles

Dreams are serious business in LA. Home to Hollywood, this is a city where fantastical thoughts are encouraged; a place gleefully wrapped in endless layers of modern mythology; an electrifying whirlpool of creativity: edgy art spaces, cult-status rock venues, acclaimed concert halls and thought-provoking stages, all fueling a city addicted to the weird, the wonderful and the downright scandalous.

Hollywood Boulevard (p24)
SEAN PAVONE/SHUTTERSTOCK ©

Los Angeles
Top Sights

Hollywood Boulevard & the Hollywood Walk of Fame (p24)

More stars than the night sky.

ffith Observatory & Hollywood Sign (p42)

iconic sights dominate the Hollywood Hills ridgeline.

Getty Center (p68)

Stellar art, architecture and gardens.

The Broad (p126)

A must-visit for contemporary-art

Santa Monica Pier (p90)

An absolutely unmissable landmark.

t Disney Concert Hall (p120)

re brilliant music meets virtuoso architecture.

ALEX MILLAUER/SHUTTERSTOCK ©

ice Boardwalk (p106)

re Venice Beach lets her freak
fly.

Los Angeles County Museum of Art (p74)

A vortex of art, jazz, film and culture.

Los Angeles
Local Life

*Local experiences and hidden ge.
to help you uncover the real c*

LA is more a neighborhood quilt than a traditional metropolis, so in your haste to
explore LA's best-known barrios, don't forget to sample the out-of-the-way corne
too. Hidden treasures await.

**Cruising
Echo Park**
(p52)

☑ Echo Park Lake
☑ Short Stop

**Gallery
Hopping in
Culver City**
(p86)

☑ Art Galleries
☑ Cutting-Edge
Architecture

Berlin Wall section on Wilshire Boulevard, from the Wende Museum

nhattan Beach, Beyond the Sand (p116)

each Living ☑Gastropubs

opping the Fashion District (p122)

ample Sales ☑People-watching

sadena (p138)

utdoor activities ☑Small-town charm

Other great places to experience the city like a local:

Farmers Markets in Hollywood (p33) and Santa Monica (p95)

Clifton's Republic (p132)

Amoeba Music (p39)

Grand Central Market (p121)

Griffith Park (p46)

Last Bookstore (p135)

Hollywood Bowl (p36)

Los Angeles Memorial Coliseum (p137)

Los Angeles Day Planner

Day One

Start your LA adventure by walking all over your favorite stars on the **Hollywood Walk of Fame** (p24) and pressing up against famous handprints outside **Grauman's Chinese Theatre** (p25). If movie props, costumes and history intrigue, hit the **Hollywood Museum** (p25) and lunch at **Musso & Frank Grill** (p32).

Up your chances of spotting actual celebs by hitting fashion-forward boutiques on **Melrose Ave** (p66). If your idols are more Kandinsky than Kardashian, snub the shops for the superlative **Los Angeles County Museum of Art** (p74).

After dinner at **Pump** (p60), saunter over to **Bar Marmont** (p63) for dirty martinis. Alternatively split your sides with late-night comedy at the **Laugh Factory** (p65) or party with WeHo's pretty boys and their fans at perennially popular **The Abbey** (p167).

Day Two

Time to hit rapidly evolving Downtown LA. Start with the LA's roots at **El Pueblo de Los Angeles** (p128) and catch up with the present at the stunning new **Broad** (p126) art museum.

Following lunch at **Grand Central Market** (p121), stroll down Broadway, a street dotted with beautiful heritage buildings, to the **Grammy Museum** (p126). Alternatively, explore the hip-and-creative Arts District, home to of-the-moment gallery **Hauser & Wirth** (p127).

Dine at **Otium** (p121), then catch the LA Phil at **Walt Disney Concert Hall** (p120), watch basketball at the **Staples Center** (p134) or enjoy jazz at **Blue Whale** (p134). If cocktails beckon, escape to **Clifton's Republic** (p132).

rt on time?

ve arranged Los Angeles' must-sees into these day-by-day itineraries to make
. you see the very best of the city in the time you have available.

y Three

Roll things out with a brilliant
Warner Bros Studio Tour (p176),
ping around back-lot sets and
nical departments and eyeing up
e of Hollywood's most famous movie
s. If you prefer your studio tours with
e of theme-park rides, opt for nearby
versal Studios Hollywood (p142).

Work off your lunch from **Bob's
Big Boy** (p147) by hiking **Griffith
k** (p46) up to the **Griffith Observa-**
(p42) in time to watch the sun sink
the city.

After a day surrounded by tourists, hang with the locals. If it's
lnesday, you'll have reserved tickets
atch jazz-playing Jeff Goldblum jam
banter with the crowd at **Rock-**
(p50). Catch the dulcet tones of
-status duo Marty and Elayne at the
sden (p49).

Day Four

☀ The **Getty Center** (p69) offers a
spectacular synergy of art, architecture, landscaping and views. If you'd
rather window shop and people watch,
hit **Rodeo Dr** (p58) and **Nate 'n Al** (p62)
for lunch.

☼ Switch worlds with a trip to ever-
cool-and-eclectic Venice. Stroll,
pedal or Rollerblade along the **Venice
Boardwalk** (p106), take in its street art
and hunt down unique fashion, accessories and art along **Abbot Kinney Blvd**
(p109). It's here that you'll find **Salt &
Straw** (p110), one of the city's best (and
most experimental) ice-cream artisans.

☾ Just like Route 66, wrap up your
own trip in oceanside Santa
Monica. Catch another perfect SoCal
sunset from **Santa Monica Pier** (p90)
before dinner at **Cassia** (p95), then toast
your trip at rooftop bar **Onyx** (p99).

Need to Know

For more information, see Survival Guide (p177)

Currency
US Dollar ($)

Language
English, with Spanish in wide use

Money
ATMs are widely available and credit cards are accepted in all hotels and most restaurants.

Cell Phones
International cell (mobile) phones will work with roaming. Some unlocked GSM phones will work with local SIMs.

Time
Pacific Standard Time (PST; UTC/GMT minus eight hours) Nov to mid-Mar; Pacific Daylight Savings Time (PDT; UTC/GMT minus seven hours) mid-Mar to Oct.

Plugs & Adaptors
LA area outlets demand the North American 20A/120V grounded plug.

Tipping
Tipping is considered mandatory for sit-down, full-service meals. The minimum tip should be 15-20%. Tip bartenders, too ($1 per drink will suffice).

① Before You Go

Your Daily Budget

Budget: Less than $150
► Dorm bed: $35–50
► Takeout meal: $6–15
► Free concerts and events

Midrange: $150–300
► Hotel double room: $200
► Two-course dinner and glass of wine: $
► Live music concert: $50

Top end: More than $300
► Three-star hotel: from $300
► Dinner at a destination restaurant: from $75, excluding drinks

Useful Websites

► **Discover Los Angeles** (www.discoverlos angeles.com) Reputable range of options f the official LA website.

► **Hotel Tonight** (www.hoteltonight.com) Cali-based hotel search app offering discou last-minute bookings.

► **Lonely Planet** (www.lonelyplanet.com/ usa/los-angeles/hotels) Expert author reviews, user feedback, booking engine.

Advance Planning

Three months before Book accommodat and rental car.

One month before Reserve tickets to ma performing arts and sporting events. Reg ter for tickets to a live TV-show taping.

Two weeks before Reserve tickets to th Broad art museum, the Frederick R Weis man Art Foundation and any LA Conserv ancy walking tour. Also reserve a table a top restaurants.

Arriving in Los Angeles

Angeles is more spread out than most or cities. Although vibrant downtown is er compact, the rest of LA is not. In fact, city is a quilt with several self-contained hborhoods knitted together and trans- details within and between them vary.

m Los Angeles International ort (LAX)

stination	Best Transport
lywood, Silver e	Metro bus 42, Metro Red Line
ntown	Metro Red Line, FlyAway Union Station
t Hollywood, -City	FlyAway Westwood, Metro 20/720, Metro 4
ta Monica	BBB 3
ice	BBB 3, CC 1
ver City	FlyAway Westwood, BBB 12
bank, Universal	FlyAway Union Station, Metrolink

🅰 Getting Around

Although car culture still rules LA, more and more Angelenos are relying on ever-evolving public transit options that link up and overlap throughout the region.

Ⓜ Metro & Metrolink

The Metro (☎323-466-3876; www.metro. net) subway and light rail system is ever-expanding and links downtown LA with Hollywood, Koreatown, Pasadena, Long Beach, LAX, Culver City and Santa Monica. It also connects with Metrolink light rail service to Burbank and Orange County.

🚌 Bus

The best bus services are offered by **LA's Metropolitan Transit Authority** (MTA; ☎323-466-3876; www.metro.net; fares from $1.75), which has a handy trip planner on its website, and Santa Monica's Big Blue Bus (☎310-451-5444; www.bigbluebus.com).

🚗 Taxi & Ride Hailing

Taxis are quite expensive and should only be used between nearby destinations. Less expensive on-demand car service apps **Uber** (www.uber.com) and **Lyft** (www.lyft.com) are quite popular and useful here for both short and longer trips.

🚲 Bike Sharing

LA has a number of bike-sharing programs in local neighborhoods, including Metro Bike Share (https://bikeshare.metro.net) in Downtown LA and Santa Monica–based Breeze Bike Share (www.santamonicabikeshare.com; per hour $7, monthly/annually $25/99). Pick up and return bikes at branded kiosks.

Los Angeles
Neighborhoods

Burbank & Universal City (p140)
Home to a theme park, Sushi Row and most of LA's major movie studios. It's also the birthplace of car culture and porn.
◉ Top Sights
Universal Studios

West Hollywood & Beverly Hills (p54)
Big dollars and gay fabulous, wonderful shopping, sinful eateries and terrific nightlife too. From here you can explore the entire city.

Santa Monica (p88)
Mix with the surf rats, skate punks, yoga freaks, psychics and street performers along a stretch of sublime coastline.
◉ Top Sights
Santa Monica Pier & Beach

◉ Getty Center

LAC

Santa Monica Pier & Beach ◉

Venice ◉ Boardwalk

Venice (p104)
Inhale an incense-scented whiff of Venice, a boho beach town and longtime haven for artists, New Agers and free spirits.
◉ Top Sights
Venice Boardwalk

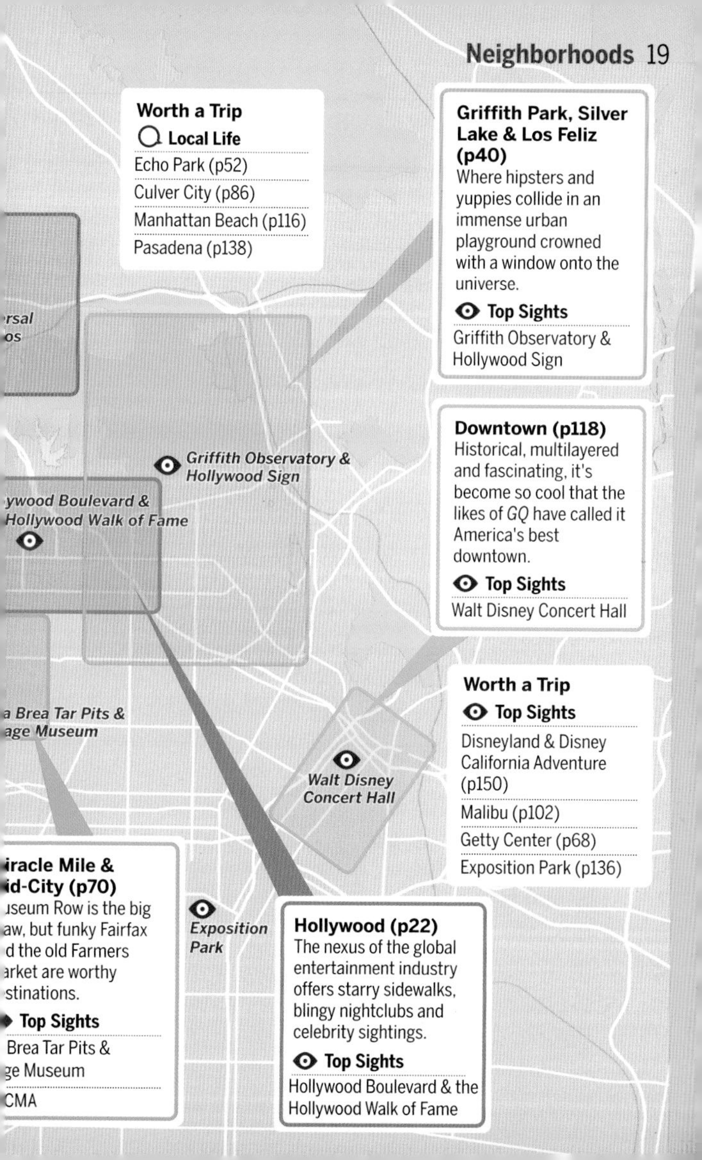

Worth a Trip

◯ Local Life

Griffith Park, Silver Lake & Los Feliz (p40)

Where hipsters and yuppies collide in an immense urban playground crowned with a window onto the universe.

⊙ Top Sights

Griffith Observatory & Hollywood Sign

Downtown (p118)

Historical, multilayered and fascinating, it's become so cool that the likes of *GQ* have called it America's best downtown.

⊙ Top Sights

Walt Disney Concert Hall

rsal
os

⊙ *Griffith Observatory & Hollywood Sign*

ywood Boulevard &
Hollywood Walk of Fame
⊙

Worth a Trip

⊙ Top Sights

a Brea Tar Pits &
age Museum

⊙
*Walt Disney
Concert Hall*

**iracle Mile &
id-City (p70)**

useum Row is the big
aw, but funky Fairfax
d the old Farmers
arket are worthy
stinations.

◉ Top Sights

Brea Tar Pits &
ge Museum

CMA

⊙
*Exposition
Park*

Hollywood (p22)

The nexus of the global entertainment industry offers starry sidewalks, blingy nightclubs and celebrity sightings.

⊙ Top Sights

Hollywood Boulevard & the Hollywood Walk of Fame

Explore
Los Angeles

View of Los Angeles from the Griffith Observatory (p42)

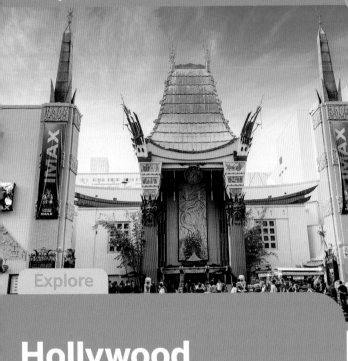

Explore

Hollywood

No other corner of LA is steeped in as much mythology as Hollywood. It's here that you'll find the Hollywood Walk of Fame, the Capitol Records Tower and Grauman's Chinese Theatre, where the hand- and footprints of entertainment deities are immortalized in concrete. Look beyond the tourist-swamped landmarks of Hollywood Blvd and you'll discover a nuanced, multifaceted neighborhood.

The Sights in a Day

☀ Start the morning with breakfast at the hip **Oaks Gourmet** (p33) before getting the insider scoop on the backlot on the **Paramount Pictures** (p28) studio tour.

☀ Most of Hollywood's main attractions are steps away from the intersection of Hollywood Blvd and Highland Ave (serviced by metro Red Line). These include **Grauman's Chinese Theatre** (p25), the **Dolby Theatre** (p25) (home of the Academy Awards), the **Egyptian Theatre** (p30), the highly recommended **Hollywood Museum** (p25) and legendary drinking hole **Musso & Frank Grill** (p32). The **Hollywood Walk of Fame** (p24) runs along Hollywood Blvd, as well as along Vine St a mile to the east, where you'll find the iconic **Capitol Records Tower** (p29).

☽ In summer, the **Hollywood Bowl** (p36) is the place to while away the evening – purchase a picnic while you watch stars on the stage beneath the stars in the sky. Anytime, suk it up at the **Upright Citizens Brigade** (p37), then linger over the skyline at **Mama Shelter's** (p34) roof bar, or catch a live band and craft cocktail at **Harvard & Stone** (p36).

 Top Sight

Hollywood Boulevard & the Hollywood Walk of Fame (p24)

♥ **Best of Los Angeles**

Eating

Musso & Frank Grill (p32)

Petit Trois (p31)

Drinking

Harvard & Stone (p36)

Entertainment

Hollywood Bowl (p36)

Fonda Theatre (p38)

Getting There

Ⓜ **Metro** The Metro Red Line has three stops along Hollywood Blvd. Most sights are convenient to Hollywood/Vine and Hollywood/Highland stations.

🚌 **Bus** Metro buses 2 and 302 run along Sunset Blvd, and buses 4 and 704 along Santa Monica Blvd. All head east to Silver Lake, Echo Park and Downtown, and west to West Hollywood, Beverly Hills and beyond.

Top Sights
Hollywood Boulevard & the Hollywood Walk of Fame

Big Bird, Bob Hope, Marilyn Monroe and Aretha Franklin are among the stars being sought out, worshipped, photographed and stepped on along the Hollywood Walk of Fame. Since 1960 more than 2600 performers – from legends to bit-part players – have been honored with a pink-marble sidewalk star. Many of Hollywood's tourist attractions gravitate around the intersection of Hollywood Blvd and Highland Ave. While many are gimmicky, there are some notable attractions here too.

Map p26, C3

www.walkoffame.com

Hollywood Blvd

M Red Line to Hollywood/Highland

Hollywood Wax Museum (p31), Hollywood Boulevard

Grauman's Chinese Theatre

Ever wondered what it's like to be in George Clooney's shoes? Just find his footprints in the forecourt of this **world-famous movie palace** (TCL Chinese Theatres; ☎323-461-3331; www.tclchinesetheatres.com; 6925 Hollywood Blvd; guided tour adult/senior/child $16/13.50/8; ♿; MRed Line to Hollywood/Highland). The exotic pagoda theater – complete with temple bells and stone heaven dogs from China – has shown movies since 1927 when Cecil B DeMille's *The King of Kings* first flickered across the screen.

Hollywood Museum

For a taste of Old Hollywood, do not miss this musty **temple to the stars** (☎323-464-7776; www.thehollywoodmuseum.com; 1660 N Highland Ave; adult/child $15/5; ☉10am-5pm Wed-Sun; MRed Line to Hollywood/Highland), its four floors crammed with movie and TV costumes and props. The museum is housed inside the Max Factor Building, built in 1914 and relaunched as a glamorous beauty salon in 1935. At the helm was Polish-Jewish businessman Max Factor, Hollywood's leading authority on cosmetics. And it was right here that he worked his magic on Hollywood's most famous screen queens.

Dolby Theatre

The Academy Awards are handed out at the **Dolby Theatre** (☎323-308-6300; www.dolbytheatre.com; 6801 Hollywood Blvd; tours adult/child, senior & student $23/18; ☉10:30am-4pm; P; MRed Line to Hollywood/Highland), which has also hosted the American Idol finale, the ESPY Awards and the Daytime Emmy Awards. The venue is home to the annual PaleyFest, the country's premier TV festival, held in March. Guided tours of the theater will have you sniffing around the auditorium, admiring a VIP room and nosing up to an Oscar statuette.

☑ **Top Tips**

▶ You can explore the boulevard by day, but it feels so much richer at night when the stars glitter and the sidewalk stains are (somewhat) hidden.

▶ New stars are born every two to three months, and include a public unveiling by the stars themselves.

✗ **Take a Break**

One of the oldest dive bars in Hollywood, the **Frolic Room** (☎323-462-5890; 6245 Hollywood Blvd; ☉11am-2am; MRed Line to Hollywood/Vine) remains a hit with local imbibers. Former regulars here included Frank Sinatra, Judy Garland and John Belushi. Select a tune on the jukebox and get friendly with the barkeeps.

For reviews see
- ◉ Top Sights   p24
- ◎ Sights   p28
- ✖ Eating   p31
- ◍ Drinking   p34
- ✪ Entertainment   p36
- ⌂ Shopping   p39

Runyon Canyon Park

Hollywood Blvd W

Cahuenga Blvd W

N Cahuenga Blvd

Hollywood Fwy

Hollywood Bowl Rd

33 ✪

Camrose Dr

WHITLEY HEIGHTS

Grace Ave

Hillcrest Rd

Sycamore

22 ✖ Scenic Gardens

Los Angeles Visitor Information Center

Franklin Ave

Franklin Ave

Whitley Ave

Yucca

Franklin Ave

N Fuller Ave

TMZ Celebrity Tour

Hollywood/ Highland

Museum of Broken Relationships

12 ◎ ◎ 2 ⓜ 3 ◎   5   16 ✖ 29 ⌂   Cos

Madame Tussaud's   Hollywood Blvd

Hollywood Walk of Fame ◎ 8 14 ◎ ◎ ◎   Egyptian   28 ⌂
                                   13 ◎   7 Theatre   37 ✪

El Capitan Theatre   Selma Ave

Ripley's Believe It or Not!   Guinness   Red Line   25 ✪
                          39 ✪   World   Tours   23 ✖
                                   Records   W Sunset Blvd
                                   Museum   40

N Gardner St
N Martel Ave
N Fuller Ave

N Gardner St
N Vista St
N Martel Ave
N Fuller Ave
N Poinsettia Pl
N Alta Vista Blvd
N Formosa Ave
N Detroit St
N La Brea Ave
N Orange Dr
N Mansfield Ave
N Highland Ave

27 ⌂

De Longpre Ave

Delongpre Park

Homeland Ave

Fountain Ave

Plummer Park

Kohn Gallery 10 ◎

Lexington Ave

Hollywood Recreation Center

17 ✖ ✖ 24

Santa Monica Blvd

Regen Projects

Warner Hollywood Studios

◎ 9
◎ 42

Hollywood Recreation Center

N Vista St
N Poinsettia Pl
Poinsettia Recreation Center

N Orange Dr
N Mansfield Ave

N Highland Ave
N Sycamore Ave

Romaine St

N Hudson Ave
Wilcox Ave
Cole Ave

⌂ 41

Willoughby Ave

✖ 15

E F G H

Griffith Park

1

HOLLYWOOD HILLS

500 m
0.25 miles

2

N Beachwood Dr

N Gower St

Argyle Ave

N Bronson Ave

21 ⊗
34 ✪

Franklin Ave

Canyon Dr

N Van Ness Ave

Taft Ave

N Wilton Pl

Garfield Pl

N Western Ave

Franklin Ave

Russell Ave

N Kingsley Dr

Hollywood Fwy

Yucca St

Hollywood Fwy

Carlos Ave

Capitol Records Tower
6

36 ✪

Hollywood/Vine
11 ⊙

38 ✪

ywood Vine
32 ⊙

Carlton Way

30 ⊙

N Kingsley Dr

N Hobart Blvd

N Serrano Ave

Hollywood Blvd

N St Andrews Pl

Hollywood/ Western
Ⓜ

W Sunset Blvd

3

YWOOD

Afton Pl

N Gower St

N Beachworth Dr

Gordon St

Tamarind Ave

N Bronson Ave

N Van Ness Ave

N St Andrews Pl

La Mirada Ave

Fountain Ave

20 ⊗

4

Lexington Ave

Lexington Ave

Virginia Ave

31 ⊙

Virginia Ave

N Oxford Ave

Santa Monica Blvd

Eleanor Ave

Beth Olam Memorial Park

4 ✪
Hollywood Forever Cemetery

N Ridgewood Pl

Lemon Grove Recreation Center

5

1 ⊙
▼

Sights

Paramount Pictures
TOURS

1 Map p26, E5

Star Trek, Indiana Jones and *Shrek* are among the blockbusters that originated at Paramount, the country's second-oldest movie studio and the only one still in Hollywood proper. Two-hour tours of the studio complex are offered year-round, taking in the back lots and sound stages. Guides are usually passionate and knowledgeable, offering fascinating insight into the studio's history and the movie-making process in general. (☏323-956-1777; www.paramountstudiotour.com; 5555 Melrose Ave; tours from $55; ⊙tours 9:30am-5pm, last tour 3pm)

TMZ Celebrity Tour
BUS

2 Map p26, C3

Cut the shame; we know you want to spot celebrities, glimpse their homes and laugh at their dirt. Join this super fun tour imagined by the paparazzi made famous. Tours run for two hours and you'll likely meet some of the TMZ stars...and perhaps even celebrity guests on the bus. (☏844-869-8687; www.tmz.com/tour; 6925 Hollywood Blvd; adult/child $54/44; ⊙tours departing Hard Rock Cafe Hollywood 12:15pm, 3pm & 5:30pm Thu-Tue, 12:15pm & 3pm Wed; Ⓜ Red Line to Hollywood/Highland)

Museum of Broken Relationships
MUSEUM

3 Map p26, C3

The everyday-looking items in this museum – clothing, perfume bottles, stuffed animals, silicone breast implants – take on entirely new meanings when you read the descriptions by their donors – emotion-filled stories of relationships that are no more. Some are wistful, others poignant, others make you want to wince. About 100 pieces – and 100 stories – are on display at any one time, and there's a confessional booth should you want to tell your own. Admission isn't cheap, but maybe emotions shouldn't be either. (☏323-892-1200; http://broken ships.la; 6751 Hollywood Blvd; adult/student & senior $18/15; ⊙11am-6pm Mon-Wed, to 7pm Thu & Sun, noon-8pm Fri & Sat; Ⓜ Red Line to Hollywood/Highland)

Hollywood Forever Cemetery
CEMETERY

4 Map p26, F5

Paradisiacal landscaping, vainglorious tombstones and epic mausoleums set an appropriate resting place for some of Hollywood's most iconic dearly departed. Residents include Cecil B DeMille, Mickey Rooney, Jayne Mansfield, punk rockers Johnny and Dee Dee Ramone and *Golden Girls* star Estelle Getty. Valentino lies in the Cathedral Mausoleum (open from 10am to 2pm), while Judy Garland rests in the Abbey of the Psalms. For a full list

Capitol Records Tower

f residents, purchase a map ($5) at he flower shop. (📞 323-469-1181; www. ollywoodforever.com; 6000 Santa Monica lvd; ⏲ usually 8:30am-5pm, flower shop am-5pm Mon-Fri, to 4pm Sat & Sun; 🅿)

Red Line Tours
WALKING

 Map p26, C3

earn the secrets of Hollywood on Red ine's 'edutaining' Hollywood Behind-he-Scenes Tour, a 75-minute walking our that comes with nifty headsets to ut out traffic noise. Guides use a mix f anecdotes, fun facts, trivia and his-orical and architectural data to keep heir charges entertained. (📞323-402-074; www.redlinetours.com; 6708 Hollywood lvd; adult/child from $25/15; ⏲75min Holly-

wood Behind-the-Scenes Tour 10am, noon, 2pm & 4pm; Ⓜ Red Line to Hollywood/Highland)

Capitol Records Tower
LANDMARK

 Map p26, E3

You'll have no trouble recognizing this iconic 1956 tower, one of LA's great mid-century buildings. Designed by Welton Becket, it resembles a stack of records topped by a stylus blinking out 'Hol-lywood' in Morse code. Some of music's biggest stars have recorded hits in the building's basement studios, among them Nat King Cole, Frank Sinatra and Capitol's current heavyweight, Katy Perry. Outside on the sidewalk, Garth Brooks and John Lennon have their stars. (1750 Vine St; admission free)

Egyptian Theatre

LANDMARK

7 Map p26, C3

The Egyptian, the first of the grand movie palaces on Hollywood Blvd, premiered *Robin Hood* in 1922. The theater's lavish getup – complete with hieroglyphs and sphinx heads – dovetailed nicely with the craze for all things Egyptian sparked by the discoveries of archaeologist Howard Carter. These days it's a shrine to serious cinema thanks to the nonprofit American Cinematheque. (☎323-461-2020; www.egyptiantheatre.com; 6712 Hollywood Blvd; Ⓜ Red Line to Hollywood/Highland)

El Capitan Theatre

LANDMARK

8 Map p26, C3

Spanish Colonial meets East Indian at the flamboyant El Capitan movie palace, built for live performances in 1926 and now run by Disney. The first flick to show here was *Citizen Kane* in 1941 and it's still an evocative place to catch a film, often accompanied by a

> Local Life
> ### Canyon Trails
> Increase your daily steps with a hike or jog through **Runyon Canyon** (www.runyoncanyonhike.com; 2000 N Fuller Ave; ⏾ dawn-dusk). Its trails are highly popular with calorie-counting locals, among them Hollywood celebrities. (And you were wondering why one of the three main trails is called the Star Trail.)

live show. (☎800-347-6396; https://elcapitantheatre.com; 6838 Hollywood Blvd)

Regen Projects

GALLERY

9 Map p26, C5

A standout private gallery, known for propelling the careers of some of LA's most successful and innovative artists, among them Matthew Barney, Glenn Ligon and Catherine Opie. Its stable also includes a number of international big guns, from Anish Kapoor to Wolfgang Tillmans. Expect bold, edgy shows showcasing everything from photography, painting and video art, to ambitious installations. (☎310-276-5424; www.regenprojects.com; 6750 Santa Monica Blvd; admission free; ⏾10am-6pm Tue-Sat)

Kohn Gallery

GALLERY

10 Map p26, C4

One of the city's top private gallery spaces, with museum-standard exhibitions of modern and contemporary art. Recent shows have included a retrospective of American conceptual artist Joe Goode and painter John Altoon, as well as the premiere of a digitally restored version of Bruce Conner's seminal experimental short film, *A Movie*. (☎323-461-3311; www.kohngallery.com; 1227 N Highland Ave; ⏾10am-6pm Tue-Fri, from 11am Sat; Ⓟ)

Hollywood & Vine

LANDMARK

11 Map p26, E3

If you'd turned on the radio in the 1920s and '30s, chances were you'd

ear a broadcast 'brought to you from
ollywood and Vine. Thanks to a
ega development splurge, including
W Hotel, a metro stop and occa-
onal block parties hosted by Jimmy
immel Live, this revitalized corner is
king a bow once more. (**M**Red Line to
ollywood/Vine)

ladame Tussaud's   MUSEUM

2 Map p26, B3

he better of Hollywood's two wax
useums, this is the place to take
lfies with motionless movie stars
alma Hayek, Tom Hanks and Patrick
wayze), old-school icons (Charlie
haplin, Marilyn Monroe, Clark
able), movie characters such as
ugh's Wolverine from *X-Men*, chart-
pping pop stars and all-time-great
rectors. To save money, book online
nd opt for the 'Late Night Saver' op-
on (adult/child $14.95/11.45), which
ants entry after 4pm. (☏323-798-
70; www.madametussauds.com; 6933
ollywood Blvd; adult/child $31/26; ☺10am-
m Mon, to 7pm Tue-Fri, to 8pm Sat & Sun;
); **M**Red Line to Hollywood/Highland)

uinness World ecords Museum   MUSEUM

3 Map p26, C3

ou know the drill: the Guinness is all
bout the fastest, tallest, biggest, fat-
st and other superlatives. Frankly it's
n underwhelming tourist trap. If you
o insist on visiting, you'll get better
alue by opting for the combination
cket (adult/child $30/18), which in-

cludes entry to the nearby **Hollywood
Wax Museum** (☏323-462-5991; www.holly
woodwax.com; 6767 Hollywood Blvd; adult/
child $20/10; ☺9am-midnight Sun-Thu, to
1am Fri & Sat;) and Ripley's Believe It
or Not! (☏323-463-6433; www.guinness
museumhollywood.com; 6764 Hollywood
Blvd; adult/child $20/10; ☺9am-midnight
Sun-Thu, to 1am Fri & Sat; ; **M**Red Line to
Hollywood/Highland)

Ripley's Believe It or Not!   MUSEUM

14 Map p26, C3

Life's pretty strange and it'll feel stranger still after you've visited Ripley's,
where exhibits range from the gross
to the grotesque. If shrunken heads,
a sculpture of Marilyn Monroe made
from shredded $1 bills and a human-
hair bikini capture your imagination,
this place is calling your name. (www.
ripleys.com/hollywood; 6780 Hollywood Blvd;
adult/child $20/10; ☺10am-midnight; **M**Red
Line to Hollywood/Highland)

Eating

Petit Trois   FRENCH $$

15 Map p26, C5

Good things come in small packages...
like tiny, no-reservations Petit Trois!
Owned by acclaimed TV chef Ludovic
Lefebvre, its two long counters (the
place is too small for tables) are where
food lovers squeeze in for smashing,
honest, Gallic-inspired grub, from
a ridiculously light Boursin-stuffed

Local Life

Thai Town

America's largest Thai Town is along Hollywood Boulevard in East Hollywood. For a transporting taste of southern Thailand, friendly **Jitlada** (☏323-667-9809; http://jitladala.com; 5233 W Sunset Blvd; mains $12-40; ☺11am-3pm & 5-10:30pm Tue-Sun; P) peddles palate-pleasing crab curry and fried *som tum* (fried papaya salad); customers include Ryan Gosling and Natalie Portman. At **Bhan Kanom** (☏323-871-8030; www.bhankanomthai.com; 5271 Hollywood Blvd; ☺10am-midnight; MRed Line to Hollywood/Western), stock up on Thai desserts, including candy, dried fruit, gummies, sours, crisps and cakes.

omelette to a showstopping double cheeseburger served with a standout foie gras–infused red-wine Bordelaise. Credit-card payment only. (☏323-468-8916; http://petittrois.com; mains $14-36; ☺noon-10pm Sun-Thu, to 11pm Fri & Sat; P)

Musso & Frank Grill STEAK $$

16 🍴 Map p26, C3

Hollywood history hangs in the thick air at Musso & Frank Grill, Tinseltown's oldest eatery (since 1919). Charlie Chaplin used to knock back vodka gimlets, Raymond Chandler penned scripts in the high-backed booths, and movie deals were made on the old phone at the back (the booth closest to the phone is favored by Jack Nicholson and Johnny Depp). (☏323-467-7788; www.mussoandfrank.com 6667 Hollywood Blvd; mains $15-52; ☺11am-11pm Tue-Sat, 4-9pm Sun; P; MRed Line to Hollywood/Highland)

Salt's Cure MODERN AMERICAN $

17 🍴 Map p26, C4

Wood-paneled, concrete-floored Salt's Cure is an out, proud locavore. From the in-season vegetables to the house-butchered and cured meats, the menu celebrates all things California. Expect sophisticated takes on rustic comfort grub, whether it's *capicollo* with chili paste or tender duck breast paired with impressively light oatmeal griddle cakes and blackberry compote (☏323-465-7258; http://saltscure.com; 1155 N Highland Ave; mains $17-34; ☺11am-11pm Mon-Thu, to midnight Fri, 10am-midnight Sat 10am-11pm Sun)

Stout Burgers & Beers BURGERS

18 🍴 Map p26, D3

Cool, casual Stout flips gourmet burgers and pours great craft brews. The beef is ground in-house, the chicken is organic and the veggie patties are made fresh daily. One of our favorites here is the Six Weeker, a beef-patty burger jammed with brie, fig jam, arugula and caramelized onions. (☏323-469-3801; www.stoutburgersandbeers.com; 1544 N Cahuenga Blvd; burgers $11-13, salads $8-12; ☺11:30am-4am; P 🛜 ; MRed Line to Hollywood/Vine)

Musso & Frank Grill

Hollywood Farmers Market

MARKET $

19 Map p26, D3

On the shortlist for the city's best farmers market, this Sunday-morning sprawl offers organic and specialty produce from well over 100 local farmers, producers and artisans. Some of the city's top chefs shop here and the market also peddles decent ready-to-eat bites for the peckish. (http://hfm.; cnr Ivar & Selma Aves; ⊙8am-1pm Sun; ⚹; Ⓜ Red Line to Hollywood/Vine)

Square One

CAFE $

20 Map p26, H4

In the shadow of the looming Scientology campus is this homely breakfast and lunch spot, complete with quirky egg-carton ceiling. Indeed, eggs feature prominently on the all-day-breakfast menu, from braised mustard and collard greens served with baked eggs and grits, to tacos filled with scrambled eggs and jalapeños. Check the board for specials such as lemon ricotta pancakes and creative salads. (☎323-661-1109; www.squareonedining.com; 4854 Fountain Ave; mains $11-15; ⊙8:30am-3pm)

Oaks Gourmet

DELI $

21 Map p26, F2

A hipster deli and wine shop with a devoted following, where you can browse Californian wines, specialty bottled cocktails, artisanal cheeses and other gourmet treats while waiting for your crowd-pleasing BLT (heirloom tomato, creamy Camembert cheese, avocado and black-forest bacon on toasted sourdough). The breakfast burrito is special. (☎323-871-8894; www.theoaksgourmet.com; 1915 N Bronson Ave; mains $9-13; ⏱7am-midnight; 🅿🛜)

Yamashiro Farmers Market

MARKET $

22 Map p26, B2

The best farmers market views in LA are yours from Yamashiro's spectacular perch. In addition to organic produce, expect tasty prepared food and live music. There's also a wine-tasting bar. (http://yamashirohollywood.com/farmers-market; 1999 N Sycamore Ave; ⏱5-9pm Thu mid-May–early Sep; 🅿)

Life Food Organic

VEGETARIAN $

23 🍴 Map p26, D3

If you're done with the tacos and cocktails, detox at this little health shop and eatery. Slurp on an almond-milk chocolate shake and fill up on the likes of turmeric-and-quinoa salads, veggie chili burgers and chocolate cream pie. Some of it might sound naughty, but everything on the menu is raw, vegetarian and nutritious. (☎323-466-0927; www.lifefoodorganic.com; 1507 N Cahuenga Ave; dishes $7-14; ⏱7:30am-9pm; 🛜)

La Carmencita

MEXICAN $$

24 🍴 Map p26, C4

Colorful, affable La Carmencita peddles delicious, made-from-scratch

Baja Californian grub. Go easy on the house-made blue-corn tortilla chips as you'll need space for the vibrant ceviche and hearty shrimp *cazuela*, a creamy, peppery, stew-like dish topped with a cheesy baked crust. Best of the tacos are the rich, succulent lamb and generous battered fish. (☎323-701-206 www.lacarmencitala.com; 1156 N Highland Ave; tacos $4.50-6; dishes $8-16; ⏱11am-11pm Mon-Sat; 🛜)

Drinking

Rooftop Bar at Mama Shelter

BA

25 🍷 Map p26, D3

Less a hotel rooftop bar than a lush, tropical-like oasis with killer views o the Hollywood sign and LA skyline, multicolored day beds and tongue-in cheek bar bites like a 'Trump' turkey burger. Pulling everyone from hotel guests to locals from the nearby Buzz feed and Lulu offices, it's a winning spot for languid cocktail sessions, landmark spotting and a game of Jenga Giant. (☎323-785-6600; www.ma mashelter.com/en/los-angeles/restaurants/rooftop; 6500 Selma Ave; ⏱11am-midnight; Ⓜ Red Line to Hollywood/Vine)

Sassafras Saloon

BA

26 🍷 Map p26, E4

You'll be pining for the bayou at the hospitable Sassafras Saloon, where hanging moss and life-size facades evoke sultry Savannah. Cocktails clude a barrel-aged Sazerac, while emed nights include live jazz on unday and Monday, brass bands nd acrobatics on Tuesday, burlesque nd blues on Wednesday, karaoke n Thursday and DJ-spun tunes on riday and Saturday. (☎323-467-2800; ww.sassafrashollywood.com; 1233 N Vine St; ⏱5pm-2am)

ibrary Bar COCKTAIL BAR

 Map p26, B4

voking an old hunting lodge with s timber panels, Chesterfield sofas nd mounted antlers, this handsome deaway sits off the Roosevelt Hotel's untain-studded lobby. You won't find cocktail menu here; simply tell the arkeeps what you're in the mood for d let them work their magic. (☎323-9-8888; www.thehollywoodroosevelt.com/ out/food-drink/library-bar; Roosevelt Hotel, 00 Hollywood Blvd; ⏱6pm-1am; 🛜; Ⓜ Red ne to Hollywood/Highland)

ayers Club CLUB

8 Map p26, D3

hen established stars such as the ack Keys, and even movie stars ch as Joseph Gordon-Levitt decide play secret shows in intimate virons, they come to the back room this brick-house Hollywood night-ot, where the booths are leather, e lighting moody and the music ways satisfying. (☎323-871-8233; www. cebook.com/TheSayersClub; 1645 Wilcox e; cover varies; ⏱9pm-2am Tue & Thu-Sat; Red Line to Hollywood/Vine)

No Vacancy BAR

29 Map p26, D3

If you prefer your cocktail sessions with plenty of wow factor, make a reserve online, style up (no sports-wear, shorts or logos) and head to this old shingled Victorian. A vintage scene of dark timber panels and elegant banquettes, you'll find bars in nearly every corner, tended by clever barkeeps while burlesque dancers and a tightrope walker entertain the droves of party people. (☎323-465-1902; www.novacancyla.com; 1727 N Hudson Ave; ⏱8pm-2am; Ⓜ Red Line to Hollywood/Vine)

Dirty Laundry BAR

Under a cotton-candy-pink apart-ment block of no particular import is this funky den (see 29 Map p26, D3) of musty odor, low ceilings, exposed pipes and good times. There's fine whiskey, funkalicious tunes on the

Top Tip

Dress Up or Dress Down?

Hollywood's bar scene is diverse and delicious, with a large number of venues on or just off Hollywood Blvd. You'll find everything from historic dive and cocktail bars once frequented by Hollywood legends, to velvet-rope hot spots, buzzing rooftop hotel bars and even a rum-and-cigar hideaway. Some of the more fashionable spots have dress codes or reservations-only policies, so always check ahead.

turntables and plenty of eye-candy peeps with low inhibitions. Alas, there are also velvet rope politics at work here, so reserve a table to make sure you slip through. (☎323-462-6531; http://dirtylaundrybarla.com; 1725 N Hudson Ave; ⏱10pm-2am Tue-Sat; Ⓜ Red Line to Hollywood/Vine)

Harvard & Stone BAR

30 Map p26, H3

With daily rotating craftsman whiskey, bourbon and cocktail specials, Harvard & Stone lures peeps with its live bands, solid DJs and burlesque troops working their saucy magic on Fridays and Saturdays. Think Colorado ski lodge meets steampunk industrial, with a blues and rockabilly soul. Note the dress code, which discourages shorts, shiny shirts, baggy clothes, sports gear and flip-flops. (☎323-466-6063; http://harvardandstone. com; 5221 Hollywood Blvd; ⏱8pm-2am; Ⓜ Red Line to Hollywood/Western)

La Descarga LOUNGE

31 Map p26, G4

This tastefully frayed, reservations-only rum-and-cigar lounge is a revelation. Behind the marble bar sit more than 100 types of rum from Haiti, Guyana, Guatemala and Venezuela. The bartenders mix specialty cocktails, but you'd do well to order something aged and sip it neat as you enjoy the Mambo and Son sounds and the burlesque ballerina on the catwalk.

(☎323-466-1324; www.ladescargala.com; 1159 N Western Ave; ⏱8pm-2am Tue-Sat)

Good Times At Davey Wayne's BAR

32 Map p26, E3

Enter the faux garage, walk through the refrigerator door and emerge in a dim, rocking ode to 1970s Californiction, complete with pine paneling, 'groovy' wallpaper and enough interior-design kitsch to make your sideburns explode. The draught beers are craftsman and there's a second b (housed in a camper) and barbecue on the back deck. Attracts mainly 20- to 30-something hipsters. (☎323-962-3804; www.goodtimesatdaveywaynes. com; 1611 N El Centro Ave; ⏱5pm-2am Mon-Fri, from 2pm Sat & Sun; Ⓜ Red Line to Hollywood/Vine)

Entertainment

Hollywood Bowl CONCERT VENU

33 Map p26, C1

Summers in LA just wouldn't be the same without alfresco melodies unde the stars at the Bowl, a huge natural amphitheater in the Hollywood Hills Its annual season – which usually ru from June to September – includes symphonies, jazz bands and iconic acts such as Blondie, Bryan Ferry an Angélique Kidjo. Bring a sweater or blanket as it gets cool at night. (☎32 850-2000; www.hollywoodbowl.com; 2301 N

Hollywood Bowl

hland Ave; rehearsals free, performance
ts vary; ☺ Jun-Sep)

right Citizens
igade Theatre   COMEDY

4 Map p26, F2

unded in New York by *SNL* alums
ny Poehler and Ian Roberts along
th Matt Besser and Matt Walsh, this
etch-comedy group cloned itself in
ollywood in 2005. With numerous
ghtly shows spanning anything
m stand-up comedy to improv and
etch, it's arguably the best comedy
b in town. Valet parking costs $7.
323-908-8702; http://franklin.ucbtheatre.
n; 5919 Franklin Ave; tickets $5-12)

ArcLight Cinemas   CINEMA

35 Map p26, D4

Assigned seats, exceptional celeb-
sighting potential and a varied
program that covers mainstream and
art-house movies make this 14-screen
multiplex the best around. If your
taste dovetails with its schedule, the
awesome 1963 geodesic Cinerama
Dome is a must. Bonuses: age-21-plus
screenings where you can booze it up,
and Q&As with directors, writers and
actors. Parking is $3 for four hours.
(☏323-464-1478; www.arclightcinemas.
com; 6360 W Sunset Blvd; Ⓜ Red Line to
Hollywood/Vine)

Pantages Theatre
THEATER

36 ⭐ Map p26, E3

The splendidly restored Pantages Theatre is an art-deco survivor from the Golden Age and a fabulous place to catch a hot-ticket Broadway musical. Recent shows include *An American in Paris*, *The Book of Mormon* and *Hamilton*. Tidbit: the theater hosted the Academy Awards ceremony between 1950 and 1959. (☎323-468-1770; http://hollywoodpantages.com; 6233 Hollywood Blvd; Ⓜ Red Line to Hollywood/Vine)

Hotel Cafe
LIVE MUSIC

37 ⭐ Map p26, D3

An anomaly on glittery Cahuenga Corridor, this intimate venue is the place for handmade music by message-minded singer-songwriters. It's mainly a stepping stone for newbie balladeers (a fresh-faced Adele wowed the crowd here back in 2008). Get there early and enter from the alley. Doors usually open at 6:30pm (check the website). (☎323-461-2040; www.hotelcafe.com; 1623 N Cahuenga Blvd; Ⓜ Red Line to Hollywood/Vine)

El Capitan Theatre
CINEMA

Disney rolls out family-friendly blockbusters at this movie palace (see 8 ◉ Map p26, C3), sometimes with costumed characters putting on the Ritz in live preshow routines. The best seats are on the balcony in the middle of the front row. VIP tickets ($28) allow you to reserve a seat and include popcorn and a beverage. (☎800-347-6396; www.elcapitantheatre.com; 6838 Hollywood Blvd; ♿ Ⓜ Red Line to Hollywood/Highland)

Fonda Theatre
CONCERT VENUE

38 ⭐ Map p26, E3

Dating back to the Roaring Twenties the since-restored Henry Fonda Theatre remains one of Hollywood's best venues for live tunes. It's an intimate (mostly) general-admission space with an open dance floor and balcony seating. Expect progressive bands such as The Radio Dept and Pussy Riot, groove masters like Clean Bandit and next-gen rappers like Kanye protégé Desiigner. (☎323-464-6269; www.fondatheatre.com; 6126 Hollywood Blvd; Ⓜ Red Line to Hollywood/Vine)

Catalina Bar & Grill
JAZZ

39 ⭐ Map p26, C3

It might be tucked in a ho-hum office building (enter through the garage), but once you're inside this sultry, premier jazz club all is forgiven. Expect a mix of top touring talent and emerging local acts – performers have included Roy Hargrove, Monty Alexander, Barbara Morrison, Kenny Burrell and Chick Corea. One or two shows nightly, best reserved ahead. (☎323-466-2210; www.catalinajazzclub.com; 6725 W Sunset Blvd; cover $15-40 plus dinner or 2 drinks)

Shopping

moeba Music   MUSIC

0 🔒 Map p26, D4

hen a record store not only survives
t thrives in this techno age, you
ow it's doing something right.
ip through 500,000 new and used
Ds, DVDs, videos and vinyl at this
anddaddy of music stores, which
so stocks band-themed T-shirts,
usic memorabilia, books and com-
s. Handy listening stations and the
ore's outstanding *Music We Like*
ooklet keep you from buying lemons.
(📞323-245-6400; www.amoeba.com; 6400
Sunset Blvd; ⏰10:30am-11pm Mon-Sat,
am-10pm Sun)

ust One Eye   FASHION & ACCESSORIES

1 🔒 Map p26, B5

oveted fashion and art collide at
st One Eye. This dramatic concept
ore hidden inside Howard Hughes'
rmer headquarters has racks hung
ith bold, creative, expensive threads
om big guns such as Gucci, Stella
cCartney and Brunello Cucinelli, as
ell as cognoscente labels like Beau
uci. Intriguing jewelry, eye-catching
icks and a smattering of collect-
ble furniture, sculpture and other

artworks (Warhol, anyone?) complete
the picture. (📞888-563-6858; http://
justoneeye.com; 700 Romaine St; ⏰10:30am-
7pm Mon-Sat)

JF Chen   DESIGN

42 🔒 Map p26, C5

A go-to for professional curators, celebrities and their interior decorators,
JF Chen offers two cluttered floors
of museum-quality furniture and
decorative arts from greats such as
Poul Kjaerholm, Ettore Sottsass, and
Charles and Ray Eames. There's never
a shortage of extraordinary pieces,
whether it's a mid-Century Modern
table made of cork, or a 1972 leather
armchair shaped like a giant baseball
glove. (📞323-463-4603; www.jfchen.com;
1000 N Highland Ave; ⏰10am-5pm Mon-Fri,
from noon Sat)

Counterpoint   MUSIC, BOOKS

Woodblock stacks are packed high
with used fiction, while crude ply-
wood bins are stuffed with vinyl soul,
classical and jazz at this shop (see 34
⭐ Map p26, F2). The real gems (the rare
first editions and vintage rock post-
ers) are in the collectible wing next
door. (📞323-957-7965; www.counterpoint
recordsandbooks.com; 5911 Franklin Ave;
⏰11am-11pm)

Explore

Griffith Park, Silver Lake & Los Feliz

Pimped with stencil art, inked skin and skinny jeans, Silver Lake is the epicenter of LA hipsterdom, home to revitalized modernist homes, sharing-plate menus and obscure fashion labels on boutique racks. Just west, easy-living Los Feliz – (mis)pronounced *Fee*-liz – is home to screenwriters, low-key celebrities and some legendary bars. North of Los Feliz lie the deep canyons and hiking trails of Griffith Park, whose own fabled icons include the mighty Griffith Observatory.

he Sights in a Day

☀ After a creative breakfast at **Sqirl** (p48), hike **Griffith Park** (46) up to **Griffith Observatory** (42), followed by a picnic-style lunch hiker favorite **Trails** (p43).

☀ Beat the heat and learn about the American West at the **Autry Museum** (p46). Then mosey over to Sunset Junction (intersection of Sunset and Santa Monica Blvds) to browse well-curated boutiques.

🌙 Follow a chef-driven dinner at **Wolfdown** (p47) with a flick at the **Vista** (p48) and cocktails as eternal songster duo Marty & Elayne entertain at **Dresden** (p49).

 Top Sights

Griffith Observatory & Hollywood Sign (p42)

🖤 **Best of Los Angeles**

Eating
HomeState (p47)

Drinking
Dresden (p49)

Shopping
Luxe De Ville (p50)

Spitfire Girl (p51)

Wacko (p51)

Getting There

🚌 **Bus** Metro bus lines 2, 4, 302 and 704 connect Downtown LA to Silver Lake. Routes 2 and 302 continue west to Los Feliz, Hollywood, West Hollywood, Beverly Hills and Santa Monica.

Ⓜ **Metro** Vermont/Santa Monica station on the Metro Red line lies 0.7 miles west of Silver Lake Junction. Trains continue to Los Feliz (Vermont/Sunset station), Hollywood and Universal Studios.

Top Sights
Griffith Observatory & Hollywood Sign

Two world-famous landmarks loom from either end of Griffith Park in the Hollywood Hills. LA's landmark 1935 observatory opens a window onto the universe from its perch on the southern slopes of Mt Hollywood. LA's most famous landmark, the Hollywood Sign, first appeared in the hills in 1923 as an advertising gimmick for a real-estate development called 'Hollywoodland'. Each letter is 50ft tall and made of sheet metal.

Map p44, B4

213-473-0890

www.griffithobservatory.org

2800 E Observatory Rd

admission to observatory free

noon-10pm Tue-Fri, from 10am Sat & Sun

Griffith Observatory

amuel Oschin Planetarium

or a tour of the cosmos, make time for the bservatory's planetarium. It's one of the finest the world, with a state-of-the-art Zeiss star rojector, digital projection system and high-tech luminum dome that transforms into a giant creen that feels impressively realistic. Three hows (adult/child $7/3) are offered: *Centered in the niverse* takes visitors back to the Big Bang, *Water Is Life* will have you searching for H_2O in the olar system, while *Light of the Valkyries* explores he phenomenon of the Northern Lights.

eonard Nimoy Event Horizon Theater

he lower levels were added to the observatory uring an ambitious restoration and expanion project completed in 2006. Insight into the roject, which included lifting the entire building ff its foundations, is offered in a 24-minute ocumentary screened in the Leonard Nimoy vent Horizon Theater. The short film also sheds ght on the observatory's namesake founder, riffith J Griffith.

elescopes, Views & Jimmy Dean

Not all the observatory's treasures are tucked way inside. The building's rooftop viewing latform offers prime-time views of LA, the Iollywood Hills and, yes, the city's most famous iant sign. Visitors are welcome to peer into the Zeiss Telescope on the east side of the roof, while fter dark, staff wheel additional telescopes out o the front lawn for stargazing. LA's hulking leco observatory is no stranger to the spotlight, aving made cameos in numerous movies and V shows, among them *La La Land, Terminaor, 24* and *Alias*. The film it's most associated vith, however, remains *Rebel Without a Cause*, ommemorated with a bust of James Dean on the vest side of the observatory lawn.

☑ Top Tips

▶ Head up on a clear day to make the most of the spectacular views and stargazing.

▶ If you're driving and only heading up for the views, do so on a weekday before noon (when the observatory opens) for easier parking.

▶ During opening hours, parking can be a trial, especially on weekends. Consider catching the DASH Observatory shuttle bus from Vermont/ Sunset metro station or hike up from Los Feliz below.

✖ Take a Break

There's a nondescript cafe at the observatory. If the weather is on your side, however, a better option is to follow the signposted 0.6-mile hike down to Fern Dell Rd for lunch at **Trails** (☏ 323-871-2102; 2333 Fern Dell Dr, Los Feliz; pastries $3-4, meals $5-9; ⏱ 8am-5pm; 🛜 🐾), an outdoor cafe with tasty, made-from-scratch savory grub and delicious baked treats.

1 km
0.5 miles

E

W Colorado Blvd

W Broadway

Los Feliz Blvd

Glendale Water
Reclamation
Plant

North
Atwater
Park

Los Angeles River

Golden State Fwy

D

Autry Museum of
the American West 1

Wilson
Golf
Course

2 Griffith
Park

Crystal Springs Dr

Vista del Valle Dr

Harding
Golf
Course

C

Commo
A

Griffith Park

Vermont
Canyon Rd

Roosevelt
Municipal Golf
Course

N Vermo

Mt Hollywood
(1625ft)

16

Griffith Park Dr

B

Mt Bell
(1587ft)

Mt Chapel
(1622ft)

Mt Hollywood Dr

Mulholland
Hwy

Griffith
Observatory

A

Forest Lawn
Memorial Park
& Hollywood Hills

Sennet Canyon

Brush
Canyon

Western
Canyon Dr

Mt Lee Dr
Mt Lee
(1640ft)

N Beachwood
Dr

Bronson 4
Canyon

Canyon Dr

1

2

3

4

uver side Dr

Rowena Ave ✕ 7

Silver Lake Reservoir

Micheltorena St

Griffith Park Blvd

St George St

SILVER LAKE

Silver Lake Blvd

N Benton Way

W Sunset Blvd

Reservoir St
✕ 10

Marathon St

Hyperion Ave ✕ 12

Micheltorena St

Silver Lake Blvd

Silver Lake Blvd

Effie St

Sunset Dr

Clayton Ave

Russell Ave

Melbourne Ave

Kingswell Ave

Prospect Ave

Edgecliff Dr
✕ 11

Myra Ave ⑱ 18

Sanborn Ave

Lucille Ave

Hyperion Ave

Bellevue Recreation Center

Marathon St

Marathon St

✕ 9 15

N Hoover St

N Hoover St

Hillhurst Ave

✕ 5

✕ 6

21 ⑯

N Vermont Ave

19

⑭ 14

17

Hollywood Blvd

⑳ 20

Vermont/ Sunset

Ⓜ 6

N Virgil Ave

Lexington Ave

Burns Ave

Monroe St

W Sunset Blvd
✕ 8

Hollywood Fwy

Finley Ave

Franklin Ave

LOS FELIZ

Barnsdall Art Park 3

✕ 13 9

Vermont/Santa Monica/LACC Ⓜ

Los Angeles City College

Monroe St

Los Feliz Blvd

Fountain Ave

W Sunset Blvd

Santa Monica Blvd

Romaine St

Hollywood/ Western Ⓜ

N Western Ave

Fern Del

Franklin Ave

Hollywood Fwy

Hollywood Blvd

N Bronson Ave

Hollywood Ave

Hollywood Forever Cemetery

Beth Olam

Memorial Park

Melrose Ave

Beverly Blvd

5

6

7

8

Sights

Autry Museum of the American West
MUSEUM

1 Map p44, D1

Established by singing cowboy Gene Autry, this expansive, underrated museum offers contemporary perspectives on the history and people of the American West, as well as their links to the region's contemporary culture. Permanent exhibitions explore everything from Native American traditions to the cattle drives of the 19th century and daily frontier life; look for the beautifully carved vintage saloon bar. You'll also find costumes and artifacts from famous Hollywood westerns such as *Annie Get Your Gun*, as well as rotating art exhibitions. (☏323-667-2000; www.autrynationalcenter.org; 4700 Western Heritage Way; adult/senior & student/child $14/10/6, 2nd Tue each month free; ⏱10am-4pm Tue-Fri, to 5pm Sat & Sun; P♿)

Griffith Park
PARK

2 Map p44, D2

A gift to the city in 1896 by mining mogul Griffith J Griffith, and five times the size of New York's Central Park, Griffith Park is one of the country's largest urban green spaces. It contains a major outdoor theater, the city **zoo** (☏323-644-4200; www.lazoo.org; 5333 Zoo Dr; adult/senior/child $20/17/15; ⏱10am-5pm, closed Christmas Day; P♿), an observatory (p42), two museums, golf courses, playgrounds, a **merry-go-round** (rides $2; ⏱11am-5pm daily earl Jun-Aug, Sat & Sun Sep-early Jun; P♿), 53 miles of hiking trails, Batman's caves and the Hollywood sign. (☏323-644-2050; www.laparks.org; 4730 Crystal Springs Dr; admission free; ⏱5am-10pm, trails sunrise-sunset; P♿)

Barnsdall Art Park
LANDMARK

3 Map p44, C6

Oil heiress Aline Barnsdall commissioned Frank Lloyd Wright to design this hilltop arts complex and residence in 1919. This promontory of a park offers views northwest to the Hollywood sign and northeast to the Griffith Observatory, and the crown-jewel **Hollyhock House** (☏323-913-4031; adult/student/child $7/3/free; ⏱tours 11am-4pm Thu-Sun; P), a prime example of Wright's California Romanza style. (www.barnsdall.org; 4800 Hollywood Blvd; ⓂRed Line to Vermont/Sunset)

Bronson Canyon
HIKING

4 Map p44, A3

Although most of the pretty people prefer to do their running, walking and hiking in Runyon Canyon, we always prefer Bronson. A wide fire road rises to a lookout point and links to the Hollywood sign, Griffith Park and the famed **Bronson Caves** – where scenes from the old *Batman* and *The Lone Ranger* series were shot. (☏818-243-1145; www.laparks.org; 3200 Canyon Dr; ⏱5am-10:30pm)

Eating

Jeni's Splendid Ice Creams
ICE CREAM **$**

5  Map p44, C5

Rarely short of a queue, this Ohio import scoops some of the city's creamiest, most inventive ice cream. Forget plain vanilla. Here, signature flavors include brown-butter almond brittle and a riesling poached-pear sorbet. Then there are the limited-edition offerings, which might leave you tossing up between a juniper and lemon-curd combo, or a spicy Queen City Cayenne. Tough gig. (☎323-928-2668; https://jenis.com; 1954 Hillhurst Ave; 2/3/4 flavors $5.50/6.50/7.50; ⊙11am-11pm)

HomeState
TEX-MEX **$**

6  Map p44, C6

Texan expat Briana Valdez is behind this rustic ode to the Lone Star State. Locals queue patiently for authentic breakfast tacos such as the Trinity, a handmade flour tortilla topped with egg, bacon, potato and cheddar. Then there's the *queso* (melted cheese) and our lunchtime favorite, the brisket sandwich, a coaxing combo of tender meat, cabbage slaw, guacamole and pickled jalapeños in pillow-soft white bread. (☎323-906-1122; www.myhomestate.com; 4624 Hollywood Blvd; tacos $3.50, dishes $7-10; ⊙8am-3pm; Ⓜ Red Line to Vermont/Sunset)

Griffith Park

Wolfdown
MODERN AMERICAN **$$$**

7  Map p44, E5

Young Korean-American chef Jason Kim has created a buzz with his latest venture, a snug, discreet restaurant with a 'deconstructed farmhouse' design, adorable outdoor patio and convivial pine-clad bar (the best seat in the house). Kim personally picks his market produce, creating seductive dishes like coconut black rice with oil-cured vegetables and a crunchy, sweet Korean fried chicken (opt for the chili version). (☎323-522-6381; www.wolfdownla.com; 2764 Rowena Ave; dishes $8-45; ⊙5:30-10pm Tue-Thu, to 11pm Fri & Sat; 🐾)

Sqirl
CAFE **$**

8 Map p44, C8

Despite its somewhat obscure location, this tiny, subway-tiled cafe is forever pumping thanks to its top-notch, out-of-the-box breakfast and lunch offerings. Join the queue to order made-from-scratch wonders such as long-cooked chicken and rice porridge served with dried lime, ginger, turmeric, cardamon ghee and tomato, or the cult-status ricotta toast, a symphony of velvety house-made ricotta, thick-cut 'burnt' brioche and Sqirl's artisanal jams. (📞323-284-8147; http://sqirlla.com; 720 N Virgil Ave; dishes $5-15; ⊙6:30am-4pm Mon-Fri, from 8am Sat & Sun; 🛜✎; Ⓜ Red Line to Vermont/Santa Monica)

Mess Hall
PUB FOOD **$$**

9 🍴 Map p44, C5

What was formerly The Brown Derby, a swing dance spot made famous by the film *Swingers,* is now a handsome,

cabin-style hangout with snug booths, TV sports and a comfy, neighborly vibe. The feel-good factor extends to the menu, with standouts that include comforting mac-n-cheese and smoky baby-back ribs with slaw and house fries. (📞323-660-6377; www.messhallkitchen.com; 4500 Los Feliz Blvd; mains $16-35; ⊙9am-10pm Sun-Thu, to 11pm Fri & Sat; Ⓟ🛜)

Elf Cafe
VEGETARIAN **$$**

10 🍴 Map p44, E8

This intimate mainstay of Echo Park (east of Silver Lake) is one of the best vegetarian restaurants in LA. The menu has distinct Mediterranean and Middle Eastern leanings, evident in thoughtful dishes such as baked feta wrapped in grape leaves and a gorgeous mushroom *kofta* with preserved lemon purée and herbed saffron yogurt. (📞213-484-6829; www.elfcafe.com; 2135 Sunset Blvd; mains $16-23; ⊙6-11pm Mon-Sat; ✎)

Kettle Black
ITALIAN **$$**

11 🍴 Map p44, D7

Kettle Black belongs to the new Silver Lake guard, a dark, stylish cocktail bar–restaurant with fashionable diners, communal bar tables and a dizzying back bar lined with clued-in craft spirits. The wood-fired oven delivers gorgeous, dense pizzas and the house-made pastas are superb. The enlightened wine list is an all-Italian affair, though we suggest an invigorating G&T made with local Mulholland Distilling gin. (📞323-641-3705; www.kettleblackla.com; 3705 W Sunset Blvd; pizzas

---

Local Life
Vista Theatre

Dating back to 1923, the single-screen **Vista** (📞323-660-6639; www.vintagecinemas.com/vista; 4473 W Sunset Blvd, Los Feliz; Ⓜ Red Line to Vermont/Sunset) has a wonderfully kitsch 'ancient Egyptian' interior and, out front, a humbler, more indie-orientated version of Hollywood's Chinese Theatre (p25) forecourt, with the concrete imprints of names such as Spike Jonze.

$13-18, mains $23-26; ⌚5-10:45pm Sun-Wed, :o 1:15am Thu-Sat)

Casita del Campo MEXICAN $$

12 Map p44, D6

What's not to love about this '60s-hrowback cantina? It's cozy, it's fun and it makes a mean, off-the-menu *amarones a la diabla* (shrimp in picy sauce). Lurking downstairs is he tiny **Cavern Club Theater** (www.avernclubtheater.com). Famed for its drag hows, its guest acts occasionally in-lude *Wigstock: The Movie* diva Jackie Beat. (☎323-662-4255; www.casitadelcampo.net; 1920 Hyperion Ave; mains lunch $10-19, dinner $13-21; ⌚11am-11pm Sun-Wed, to midnight Thu, to 2am Fri & Sat; P 📶)

Drinking

The Virgil BAR

13 Map p44, C7

An atmospheric, vintage-styled neigh-borhood hangout serving craftsman ocktails to local hipsters and arty ypes. A stocked calendar of entertain-nent includes top-notch live-comedy ights, including hilarious, subversive rotic fan-fiction improv on the third unday of the month. Other rotating vents include booze-fueled spelling ees, storytelling events, bands and hemed club nights, including '80s-hemed Funkmosphere on Thursdays. Did we mention the jukebox? (☎323-60-4540; www.thevirgil.com; 4519 Santa Monica Blvd; ⌚7pm-2am)

Dresden COCKTAIL BAR

14 Map p44, C6

Marty and Elayne have been a Los Feliz fixture since 1982 when they first brought their quirky Sinatra style to the Dresden's mid-century lounge. He rumbles on the drums and the upright bass; she tickles the ivories and plays the flute. Both sing. Their fame peaked when they made a brief appearance in the film *Swingers*. (☎323-665-4294; www.thedresden.com; 1760 N Vermont Ave; ⌚4:30pm-2am Mon-Sat, to midnight Sun; M Red Line to Vermont/Sunset)

Tiki-Ti BAR

15 Map p44, D6

Channeling Waikiki since 1961, this tiny tropical tavern packs in everyone from Gen-Y hipsters to grizzled old-timers in 'nonironic' Hawaiian shirts. Drinks are strong and smooth; order the tequila-fueled Blood and Sand and expect a ritual that involves raucous cheers and a charging bull. The brown-paper tags are notes written by regulars, some of them dating back to the '60s. (☎323-669-9381; www.tiki-ti.com; 4427 W Sunset Blvd; ⌚4pm-2am Wed-Sat)

Entertainment

Greek Theatre LIVE MUSIC

16 Map p44, C4

The 'Greek' in the 2010 film *Get Him to the Greek* is this 5900-capacity outdoor amphitheater, tucked into a

Local Life
VintageVille

Los Feliz, Silver Lake and neighboring Echo Park burst with vintage stores. Standouts like **Luxe de Ville** (☎213-353-0135; http://luxedeville.com; 2157 Sunset Blvd; ⏲12:30-7pm Mon, from noon Tue-Sat, noon-5pm Sun), **Lemon Frog** (☎213-413-2143; http://lemonfrogshop.com; 1202 N Alvarado St; ⏲10:30am-5:30pm Mon-Wed & Sat, to 6:30pm Thu, 11:30am-7:30pm Fri, noon-5pm Sun), **Foxhole LA** (☎213-290-7175; www.foxholela.com; 3318 W Sunset Blvd; ⏲noon-5pm Mon-Sat) and **SquaresVille** (☎323-669-8464; www.squaresvillevintage.com; 1800 N Vermont Ave; ⏲noon-7pm Mon & Sun, 11am-8pm Tue-Thu, 11am-9pm Fri & Sat) will turn you into a hipster hottie.

woodsy Griffith Park hillside. A more intimate version of the Hollywood Bowl, it's much loved for its vibe and variety – recent acts include PJ Harvey, John Legend and Pepe Aguilar. Parking (cash only) is stacked, so plan on a post-show wait. (☎844-524-7335; www.lagreektheatre.com; 2700 N Vermont Ave; ⏲Apr-Oct)

Rockwell   LIVE MUSIC

17 ⭐ Map p44, C6

If you like to be entertained while you chew, come to this table and stage. Make a reservation for Wednesday night, when Jeff Goldblum and his Mildred Snitzer Orchestra usually take to the stage. The Hollywood veteran knows how to charm his crowd, encouraging selfies with the star. (☎323-669-1550; http://rockwell-la.com; 1714 N Vermont Ave; Ⓜ Red Line to Vermont/Sunset)

Shopping

Mohawk General Store   FASHION & ACCESSORIES

18 🔒 Map p44, D7

Stylish individualists hit Mohawk for edgy, progressive men's fashion and accessories, including hard-to-find fragrances from the likes of Byredo and jewelry by local designer Matthew Ready. Fashion-forward labels include Belgium's Jan-Jan Van Essche and Mohawk's own Smock. The mezzanine level is dedicated to Dries Van Noten and, unexpectedly, a small collection of vintage hi-fi equipment. (☎323-669-1602; www.mohawkgeneralstore.com; 4017 W Sunset Blvd; ⏲11am-7pm Mon-Sat, to 6pm Sun)

Steven Alan Outpost   FASHION & ACCESSORIES

The fashion cognoscenti love New York designer Steven Alan for his super-cute men's and women's threads, which fuse preppy style with unique detailing and effortless casual cool. And it's here, at his Los Feliz outpost (see 21 🔒 Map p44, C5), that you can bag his shirts, tees, trousers, dresses, skirts and bags at heavily discounted prices. (☎323-667-9500; www.stevenalan.com; 1937 Hillhurst Ave; ⏲11am-7pm Mon-Sat, to 6pm Sun)

Skylight Books
BOOKS

19 🔒 Map p44, C5

Occupying two adjoining shopfronts, this much-loved Los Feliz institution carries everything from art, architecture and fashion tomes, to LA history titles, vegan cookbooks, queer literature and critical theory. There's a solid selection of niche magazines and local zines, some great lit-themed tees and regular, engaging in-store readings and talks (with the podcasts uploaded onto the store's website). (📞323-660-1175; www.skylightbooks.com; 1818 N Vermont Ave; ⏰10am-10pm)

Wacko
COLLECTIBLES

20 🔒 Map p44, C6

Billy Shire's giftorium of camp and kitsch has been a fun browse for over three decades. Pick up a *Star Wars* tote, some Gauguin socks or a Hillary Clinton paper doll. You'll find a great selection of comics and books by LA authors such as Ray Bradbury and Philip K Dick. (📞323-663-0122; www.soapplant.com; 4633 Hollywood Blvd; ⏰11am-7pm Mon-Wed, to 9pm Thu, to 10pm Fri & Sat, noon-5pm Sun; Ⓜ Red Line to Vermont/Sunset)

Spitfire Girl
GIFTS & SOUVENIRS

21 🔒 Map p44, C5

This is one of the city's coolest, quirkiest gift boutiques, where fine jewelry, art tomes, papier-mâché mounts and

Brian Aubert of Silversun Pickups performs at the Greek Theatre (p49)

aromatic candles mingle with stuffed gnomes and the odd taxidermy item. We especially love the store's unisex fragrances and handmade pillows, the latter's graphic prints ranging from 19th-century photographs to pop-art comics and quotes straight out of a drag queen's mouth. (📞323-912-1977; www.spitfiregirl.com; 1939 Hillhurst Ave; ⏰11am-7pm Mon-Fri & Sun, to 7:30pm Sat)

Local Life
Cruising Echo Park

If you dig the uneasy interface of edgy urban art, music and culture in multiethnic neighborhoods, you'll love Echo Park, punctuated by the fountain lake featured in Polanski's *Chinatown*. True, the artists and hipsters have arrived, but the *panaderías* and *cevicherías* happily remain.

Getting There

🚗 Just west of Downtown, Sunset Blvd is the main thoroughfare. You may also access Echo Park from I-101.

🚌 Metro bus line 2 serves the district.

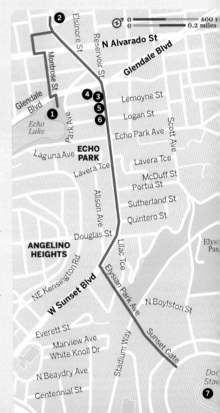

❶ Echo Park Lake

A former reservoir to homesteading families in the late 19th century, **Echo Park Lake** (www.laparks.org; 751 Echo Park Ave; ⓟ) is best known as the setting for Jake Gittes' surreptitious rowboating shenanigans in Polanski's classic film, and for its keyhole vistas toward downtown. Find the boathouse and rent a pedal boat or a canoe with the kids.

❷ IAm8Bit

Echo Park's funkiest art space, **IAm-8Bit** (☎213-908-6154; www.iam8bit.com; 2147 W Sunset Blvd; ◷5-10pm Thu & Fri, 1-10pm Sat, noon-5pm Sun) offers stellar art shows at its expansive 4500-sq-ft gallery in the heart of Echo Park.

❸ Deepest Dish

Chicago deep-dish pizza is served at **Masa** (☎213-989-1558; www.masaofecho park.com; 1800 W Sunset Blvd; pizzas from $13; ◷11am-11pm Sun-Thu, to midnight Fri & Sat; ⓟ) in whimsical environs that recall the wild, colorful swirl of New Orleans, right down to the swing music. They do brunch on weekends.

❹ Night Music

Eastsiders hungry for an eclectic alchemy of sounds pack the **Echo** (www.attheecho.com; 1822 W Sunset Blvd; cover varies). It books indie bands like Black Rebel Motorcycle Club and also has regular club nights in the larger Echoplex Theater.

❺ Stories

Bob your head to dub on the hi-fi while you wander through a mini maze of new and used literature inside **Stories** (☎213-413-3733; www.stories la.com; 1716 W Sunset Blvd; ◷8am-11pm Sun-Thu, to midnight Fri & Sat; 🛜). Score anything and everything from plays, poetry and short-story anthologies, to graphic novels, brain-twisting metaphysics titles and LA-themed books. Brainy types congregate in the back-end cafe, which comes with free wi-fi, fresh grub and a cute back patio.

❻ KindKreme

Sage (☎213-989-1718; www.sagevegan bistro.com; 1700 W Sunset Blvd; dishes $9-15; ◷11am-10pm Mon-Wed, to 11pm Thu & Fri, 9am-4pm & 5-11pm Sat, to 10pm Sun; 🛜🌿♿) is an organic vegan kitchen with sandwiches and veggie burgers, crafted with love and talent and served in heaped portions. And the menu is the second-best thing here. The best? That would be KindKreme's good-for-you, raw ice cream. Taste to believe.

❼ Dodger Stadium

Built in 1962 and one of Major League Baseball's classic ballparks, **Dodger Stadium** (☎866-363-4377; http://m.mlb. com/dodgers/tickets/tours; 1000 Elysian Park Ave; tours adult/child & senior from $20/15; ◷tours 10am, 11:30am & 1pm; ⓟ) is now offering regular behind-the-scenes tours through the press box, the Dodger dugout, the Dugout Club, the field and the Tommy Lasorda Training Center. Of course, the best way to experience it is to catch a ball game.

Explore

West Hollywood & Beverly Hills

If any two neighborhoods encapsulate the LA of international fantasies, surely they're West Hollywood and Beverly Hills. 1.9-sq-mile West Hollywood (WeHo) is both a bastion of LA's fashionista and foodie-nista best and home to some of the trashiest shops you'll ever see, plus clubs to rock the night away. Just west, Beverly Hills lures with its high-end boutiques along Rodeo Drive, palm-lined boulevards and swanky bistros filled with power-lunching movie execs.

The Sights in a Day

☀ Make like Larry King and grab a classic bagels & lox breakfast at **Nate'n Al** (p62), then head to the **Museum of Tolerance** (p58) or **Hammer Museum** (p58).

☀ Power lunch with the best of them at **the Ivy** (p61) before strolling the fashionable boutiques nearby on and around **Robertson Blvd**, then head to world capital of posh, **Rodeo Drive** (p58), for a leisurely stroll.

☾ Begin with a classic cocktail at **Bar Marmont** (p63) before dinner of groundbreaking Southeast Asian fare at **EP & LP** (p61) or gorgeous gourmet vegan Mexican at **Gracias Madre** (p61). Then laugh it up at the **Groundlings** (p65), or party all night in the gay clubs of WeHo – **the Abbey** (p63) is a good start.

 **Best of Los Angeles**

Eating
Joss Cuisine (p62)

Drinking
Bar Marmont (p63)

Polo Lounge (p64)

Shopping
Melrose Avenue (p66)

Mystery Pier Books (p66)

Book Soup (p66)

Getting There

🚌 **Bus** Metro lines 2 (along Sunset Blvd), 4 and 704 (along Santa Monica Blvd), 10 (along Melrose Ave), 14 (along Beverly Blvd) and 20 and 720 (along Wilshire Blvd) connect with neighborhoods to the east and west. From airports, your best bet is a taxi or ride-hailing app such as Uber or Lyft.

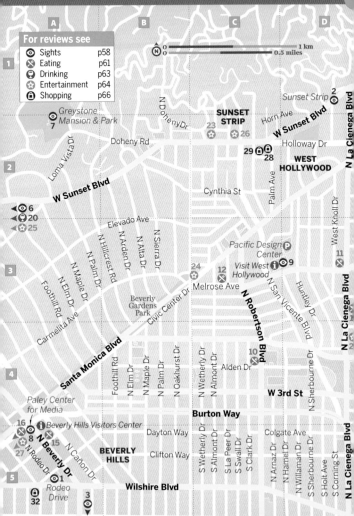

Greystone Mansion & Park 7

Doheny Rd

N Doheny Dr

Loma Vista Dr

W Sunset Blvd

SUNSET STRIP

23 26

Sunset Strip

Horn Ave

W Sunset Blvd 2

N La Cienega Blvd

Holloway Dr

29 28

WEST HOLLYWOOD

Palm Ave

Cynthia St

6
20
25

Elevado Ave

N Sierra Dr

N Alta Dr

N Arden Dr

N Hillcrest Rd

N Palm Dr

N Maple Dr

N Elm Dr

Foothill Rd

Carmelita Ave

Pacific Design Center P

Visit West Hollywood ℹ 9

West Knoll Dr

11

24

12

Melrose Ave

N San Vicente Blvd

Huntley Dr

N La Cienega Blvd

Beverly Gardens Park

Civic Center Dr

N Robertson Blvd

Santa Monica Blvd

Foothill Rd

N Elm Dr

N Maple Dr

N Palm Dr

N Oakhurst Dr

N Wetherly Dr

N Almont Dr

10

Alden Dr

W 3rd St

N Sherbourne Dr

Paley Center for Media

16
8
27

Beverly Hills Visitors Center ℹ

15

N Rodeo Dr

N Beverly Dr

N Canon Dr

Burton Way

Dayton Way

Clifton Way

BEVERLY HILLS

S Wetherly Dr

S Almont Dr

S La Peer Dr

S Swall Dr

S Clark Dr

Colgate Ave

N Arnaz Dr

N Hamel Dr

N Willaman Dr

S Sherbourne Dr

S Holt Ave

S Corning St

S La Cienega Blvd

32

Rodeo Drive

3

Wilshire Blvd

1 km
0.5 miles

E **F** **G** **H**

19

N Kings Rd

William S Hart Park

N Flores St

W Sunset Blvd

30

De Longpre Ave

N Crescent Heights Blvd

Fountain Ave

N Orange Grove Ave

N Ogden Dr

N Genesee Ave

N Vista St

N Martel Ave

N Fuller Ave

N Detroit St

WEST HOLLYWOOD

Hampton Ave

Plummer Park

Lexington Ave

Norton Ave

N La Brea Ave

Norton Ave

Santa Monica Blvd

Santa Monica Blvd

Bikes & Hikes LA

5

Romaine St

N Kings Rd

N Sweetzer Ave

N Laurel Ave

N Edinburgh Ave

N Hayworth Ave

N Fairfax Ave

N Orange Grove Ave

N Ogden Dr

N Genesee Ave

N Curson Ave

N Sierra Bonita Ave

Poinsettia Recreation Center

Willoughby St

Willoughby Ave

4

Schindler House

Waring Ave

Waring Ave

Melrose Ave

Melrose Ave

31

BEVERLY CENTER DISTRICT

Clinton St

Clinton St

MELROSE/ LA BREA

N Fairfax Ave

N Spaulding Ave

N Stanley Ave

N Curson Ave

N Gardner St

N Vista St

N Martel Ave

N Fuller Ave

N Poinsettia Pl

N Alta Vista Blvd

N Formosa Ave

N Detroit St

N La Brea Ave

Rosewood Ave

N Ogden Dr

Oakwood Ave

FAIRFAX DISTRICT

17

Beverly Blvd

S Edinburgh Ave

Beverly Blvd

MID-CITY

21

W 1st St

The Grove

Pan Pacific Park

The Grove Dr

S Gardner St

S Vista St

S Martel Ave

S Fuller Ave

S Poinsettia Pl

S Alta Vista Blvd

S Detroit St

W 1st St

S La Brea Ave

3

W 3rd St

W 3rd St

S Sweetzer Ave

Colgate Ave

S Fairfax Ave

Colgate Ave

S Curson Ave

W 4th St

1

2

3

4

5

Sights

Rodeo Drive
STREET

1 Map p56, A5

It might be pricey and unapologetically pretentious, but no trip to LA would be complete without a saunter along Rodeo Dr, the famous three-block ribbon of style where sample-size fembots browse for Gucci and Dior.

Sunset Strip
STREET

2 Map p56, D1

A visual cacophony of billboards, giant ad banners and neon signs, the sinuous stretch of Sunset Blvd running between Laurel Canyon and Doheny Dr has been nightlife central since the 1920s. (Sunset Blvd)

Local Life

Hammer Museum

Once a vanity project of the late oil tycoon Armand Hammer, this eponymous **museum** (☎310-443-7000; www.hammer.ucla.edu; 10899 Wilshire Blvd; admission free; ⏱11am-8pm Tue-Fri, to 5pm Sat & Sun; Ⓟ) has become a widely respected art space. Selections from Hammer's personal collection include relatively minor works by Monet, Van Gogh and Mary Cassatt, but the museum really shines when it comes to cutting-edge contemporary exhibits featuring local, underrepresented and controversial artists. It's in Westwood, west of Beverly Hills.

Museum of Tolerance
MUSEUM

3 Map p56, A5

Run by the Simon Wiesenthal Center, this powerful, deeply moving museum uses interactive technology to engage visitors in discussion and contemplation of racism and bigotry. Particular focus is given to the Holocaust, with a major basement exhibition that examines the social, political and economic conditions that led to the Holocaust as well as the experience of the millions persecuted. On the museum's 2nd floor, another major exhibition offers an intimate look into the life and effect of Anne Frank. (☎reservations 310-772-2505; www.museumoftolerance.com; 9786 W Pico Blvd; adult/senior/student $15.50/12.50/11.50, Anne Frank Exhibit adult/senior/student $15.50/13.50/12.50; ⏱10am-5pm Sun-Wed & Fri, to 9:30pm Thu, to 3:30pm Fri Nov-Mar; Ⓟ)

Schindler House
ARCHITECTURE

4 Map p56, E2

The former home and studio of Vienna-born architect Rudolph Schindler (1887–1953) offers a fine primer on the modernist elements that so greatly influenced mid-century California architecture. The open-floor plan, flat roof and glass sliding doors, while considered avant-garde back in the 1920s, all became design staples after WWII. (☎323-651-1510; www.makcenter.org; 835 N Kings Rd; adult/senior & student/under 12 $10/7/free, 4-6pm Fri free ⏱11am-6pm Wed-Sun; 🚇MTA line 4)

Melrose Avenue (p66)

Bikes & Hikes LA

OUTDOORS

5 Map p56, E2

This WeHo-based outfit rents bikes and offers scheduled cycling tours of Hollywood, Beverly Hills, stars' homes and the signature 32-mile 'LA in a Day' ($162) for fit cyclists, taking in celebrity homes, swank shopping streets, inspiring architecture and the Pacific. Hiking tours venture around Griffith Park (including awesome Hollywood Sign selfies) on a light-to-moderate, family-friendly hike. (☑323-796-8555; www.bikesandhikesla.com; 8250 Santa Monica Blvd; self-guided/guided tours from $39/52, bike rentals per hour/day from $8.50/32)

Frederick R Weisman Art Foundation

MUSEUM

6 Map p56, A2

The late entrepreneur and philanthropist Frederick R Weisman had an insatiable passion for art, a fact confirmed when touring his former Holmby Hills home. From floor to ceiling, the mansion (and its manicured grounds) bursts with extraordinary works from visionaries such as Picasso, Kandinsky, Miró, Magritte, Picasso, Rothko, Warhol, Rauschenberg and Ruscha. There's even a motorcycle painted by Keith Haring. Tours should be reserved at least a few days ahead. (☑310-277-5321; www.weismanfoundation. org; 265 N Carolwood Dr; admission free;

Understand
Celebrity Chefs

Greater WeHo practically boils over with celebrity chefs. Jon Shook and Vinny Dotolo's mini restaurant empire started with Animal (p80) and **Son of a Gun** (☏323-782-9033; www.sonofagunrestaurant.com; 8370 W 3rd St; dishes $8-32; ⊘noon-3pm daily, 6-10pm Sun-Thu, to 11pm Fri & Sat; ▣MTA line 16). Chef Tal Ronnen has transformed vegan cooking at Crossroads (p81). Two actual cousins parlayed appearances on TV's Shark Tank into **Cousins Maine Lobster** (☏424-204-9923; www.cousinsmainelobster.com; 8593 Santa Monica Blvd; mains $10-17; ⊘11am-10pm Tue-Sun, to 9pm Mon; ℗; ▣MTA line 4, 704), while Kris Yenbamroong breaks Thai cooking barriers at **Night + Market** (☏310-275-9724; www.nightmarketla.com; 9043 W Sunset Blvd; dishes $8-15; ⊘11:30am-2:30pm Tue-Thu, 5-10:30pm Tue-Sun), winning Food & Wine's best new chef award for 2016. Even the out-of-towners are taking notice, as New York-based Danny Meyer with **Shake Shack** (☏323-488-3010; www.shakeshack.com; 8520 Santa Monica Blvd; burgers & hot dogs $3.50-10; ⊘11am-11:30pm; ℗🍴). And speaking of celebrities, TV's Vanderpump Rules' Lisa Vanderpump is the force behind **Pump** (☏310-657-7867; www.pumprestaurant.com; 8948 Santa Monica Blvd; appetizers $14-18, salads $14-26, dinner mains $18-38, brunch mains $14-24; ⊘5pm-2am Mon-Fri, from 11:30am Sat & Sun; ℗).

⊘90min guided tours 10:30am & 2pm Mon-Fri, by appointment only)

Greystone Mansion & Park
NOTABLE BUILDING

7 ◉ Map p56, A2

Known for inducing bouts of real-estate envy, this Tudor Revival mansion dates back to 1927. Hoover Dam architect Gordon Bernie Kaufmann designed the estate, which was a generous gift from oil tycoon Edward L. Doheny to his son Ned and his family. In 1929 the oil heir was found with a bullet in his head along with his male secretary in an alleged murder-suicide – a mystery that remains unsolved to this day. (☏310-286-0119; www.greystone mansion.org; 905 Loma Vista Dr; ⊘10am-6pm mid-Mar–Oct, to 5pm Nov-early Mar; ℗)

Paley Center for Media
MUSEUM

8 ◉ Map p56, A5

The main lure of the Paley Center, located in a crisp white building by Getty Center architect Richard Meier, is its mind-boggling archive of TV and radio broadcasts dating back to 1918. The Beatles' US debut on the Ed Sullivan Show? The moon landing? All here and yours to view without the need to book ahead. The center also hosts regular discussions with the casts of hit TV shows. (☏310-786-1091; www.paleycenter.org; 465 N Beverly Dr; suggested donation adult/child $10/5; ⊘noon-5pm Wed-Sun; ℗)

Pacific Design Center LANDMARK

9 ◉ Map p56, D3

Interior design is big in WeHo, with more than 120 trade-only showrooms at the Pacific Design Center and dozens more in the surrounding **Avenues of Art & Design** (Beverly Blvd, Robertson Blvd and Melrose Ave). PDC showrooms generally sell only to design pros, but often you can get items at a mark-up through the Buying Program. (PDC; www.pacificdesign center.com; 8687 Melrose Ave; ⏱9am-5pm Mon-Fri)

Eating

The Ivy CALIFORNIAN $$$

10 🍴 Map p56, C4

Amid the modeling agencies and couture boutiques, and with a long history of celebrity power lunches, this flower-festooned and cushioned cottage is where Southern comfort food (such as fried chicken and crab cakes) has been elevated to haute cuisine. Service is refined and impeccable and paparazzi etiquette (among one another and their prey) is a fluid, dynamic beast. (📞310-274-8303; www. theivyrestaurants.com; 113 N Robertson Blvd; mains $22-97; ⏱8am-11pm; 🅿)

EP & LP SOUTHEAST ASIAN $$

11 🍴 Map p56, D3

Louis Tikaram, Australia's Chef of the Year in 2014, has brought the creative, bold flavors of his Fijian-Chinese heritage – *kakoda* (Fijian-style ceviche), Chiang Mai larb (spiced salmon stands in for meat) and crispy chicken with black vinegar, chili and lemon – to some of LA's most enviable real estate, at the corner of Melrose and La Cienega. (📞310-855-9955; http://eplos angeles.com; 603 N La Cienega Blvd; small plates $10-18, large plates $20-34; ⏱5pm-2am Mon-Fri, from noon Sat & Sun)

Gracias Madre VEGAN, MEXICAN $$

12 🍴 Map p56, C3

Gracias Madre shows just how tasty – and chichi – organic, plant-based Mexican cooking can be. Sit on the gracious patio or in the cozy interior and feel good as you eat healthy: sweet potato flautas, coconut 'bacon,' plantain 'quesadillas,' plus salads and bowls. We're consistently surprised at innovations like cashew 'cheese', mushroom 'chorizo' and heart-of-palm 'crab cakes.' (📞323-978-2170; www. graciasmadreweho.com; 8905 Melrose Ave; mains lunch $10-13, dinner $12-18; ⏱11am-11pm Mon-Fri, from 10am Sat & Sun; 🌿)

Joan's on Third CAFE $$

13 🍴 Map p56, E4

One of the first market cafes in the LA area, Joan's on Third is still one of the best. The coffee and pastries are absurdly good and the deli churns out tasty gourmet sandwiches and salads. Hence all the happy people eating alfresco on buzzy 3rd St. (📞323-655-2285; www.joansonthird.com; 8350 W 3rd St;

STEFANIE KEENAN/CONTRIBUTOR/GETTY IMAGES ©

Bar Marmont

Nate'n Al

DELI $$

15 Map p56, A5

Dapper seniors, chatty girlfriends, busy execs and even Larry King have kept this New York–style nosh spot busy since 1945. The huge menu brims with corned beef, lox, matzo-ball soup and other old-school favorites, but we're partial to the pastrami, made fresh on-site. (☎310-274-0101; www.natenal.com; 414 N Beverly Dr; dishes $7-22; ⏱7am-9pm; 🚼)

Joss Cuisine

CHINESE $$

16 Map p56, A5

With fans including Barbra Streisand, Gwyneth Paltrow and Jackie Chan, this warm, intimate nosh spot serves up superlative, MSG-free Chinese cuisine at non-celebrity prices. Premium produce drives a menu of exceptional dishes, from flawless dim sum and ginger fish broth, to crispy mustard prawns and one of the finest Peking ducks you'll encounter this side of east Asia. Reservations recommended. (☎310-277-3888; www.josscuisine.com; 9919 S Santa Monica Blvd; dishes $15-30; ⏱noon-3pm Mon-Fri, 5:30-10pm daily)

Escuela Taqueria

MEXICAN $$

17 Map p56, G4

An upscale, new-school taqueria. Vegetarians may opt for the roasted *poblano* and jack cheese tacos; fish heads will dig the branzino, shrimp or lobster (hell yes!). It also serves carnitas, and the crispy beef and pickle is its answer

mains $10-16; ⏱8am-8pm Mon-Sat, to 7pm Sun; 🖊🚼)

Connie & Ted's

SEAFOOD $$$

14 Map p56, E2

At this modernized version of a New England seafood shack by acclaimed chef Michael Cimarusti, there are always up to a dozen oyster varieties at the raw bar, classics such as fried clams, grilled fish (wild and sustainably raised), lobsters and steamers, and lobster rolls served cold with mayo or hot with drawn butter. The shellfish marinara is a sacred thing. (☎323-848-2722; www.connieandteds.com; 8171 Santa Monica Blvd; mains $13-44; ⏱4-10pm Mon & Tue, 11:30am-10pm Wed & Thu, 11:30am-11pm Fri, 10am-11pm Sat, 10am-10pm Sun; 🅿)

a burger in taco clothing. It doesn't serve alcohol, but you can bring your own for $4 per person. (☎323-932-6178; www.escuelataqueria.com; 7615 Beverly Blvd; tacos & burritos $4-12; ⏱11am-11pm)

Real Food Daily
VEGAN $$

18 ✖ Map p56, D3

Once the one-and-only tasty option for vegans, this famous kitchen from chef and cookbook author Ann Gentry still satisfies even devout carnivores with tacos, macrobiotic rice bowls and more. Produce is almost entirely organic, water is filtered and even the takeout containers are environmen-tally friendly. And she's been doing it since 1993. (☎310-289-9910; www.realfood.com; 414 N La Cienega Blvd; mains $14-18; ⏱11am-9pm Mon, to 10pm Tue-Fri, 10am-10pm Sat, 10am-9pm Sun; ✔)

Drinking

Bar Marmont
BAR

19 🍷 Map p56, E1

Elegant, but not stuck up; been around, yet still cherished. With high ceilings, molded walls and terrific martinis, the famous and the wish-they-weres still flock here. If you time

---

Understand

WeHo, SoCal's Gay Capital

West Hollywood is simply is one of the world's top spots for gay nightlife, with dozens of shops, restaurants and nightspots all along Santa Monica Blvd; the highest concentration is between Robertson Blvd and Palm Dr. **The Abbey** (☎310-289-8410; www.theabbeyweho.com; 692 N Robertson Blvd; ⏱11am-2am Mon-Thu, from 10am Fri, from 9am Sat & Sun) has been called the world's best gay bar, pulsing with go-go dancers, flavored martinis and mojitos and a multitude of indoor-outdoor spaces; it also has and its own reality TV show. **Micky's** (www.mickys.com; 8857 Santa Monica Blvd; ⏱5pm-2am Mon-Thu, to 4am Fri, 3pm-4am Sat, 2pm-2am Sun) is a quintessential WeHo dance club, with go-go boys, expensive drinks, attitude and plenty of eye candy, while nearby **Rage** (☎310-652-7055; www.ragenightclub.com; 8911 Santa Monica Blvd) does theme nights like Asian, Latin and Musical Mondays. **Fiesta Cantina** (☎310-652-8865; www.fiestacantina.net; 8865 Santa Monica Blvd; ⏱noon-2am) is the essence of cheap and cheer-ful, packing in a vibrant crowd of 20-something twinks thanks to extra-long happy hours and reasonably priced Mexican fare. The crowd skews some-what older at **Trunks** (☎310-652-1015; www.trunksbar.com; 8809 Santa Monica Blvd; ⏱1pm-2am), a brick-house, low-lit dive that's less fabulous and more down to earth than most in WeHo. And that can be a very good thing.

it right you might see celebs – the Marmont doesn't share who (or else they'd stop coming – get it?). Come midweek. Weekends are for amateurs. (☎323-650-0575; www.chateaumarmont.com; 8171 Sunset Blvd; ⏰6pm-2am)

Polo Lounge   COCKTAIL BAR

20 Map p56, A2

For a classic LA experience, dress up and swill martinis in the Beverly Hills Hotel's legendary bar. Charlie Chaplin had a standing lunch reservation at booth 1 and it was here that HR Haldeman and John Ehrlichman learned of the Watergate break-in in 1972. There's a popular Sunday jazz brunch (adult/child $75/35). (☎310-887-2777; www.dorchestercollection.com/en/los-angeles/the-beverly-hills-hotel; Beverly Hills Hotel, 9641 Sunset Blvd; ⏰7am-1:30am)

Roger Room   COCKTAIL BAR

Roger Room (see 22 ⭐ Map p56, D4) is ramped but cool; too cool even to have a sign out front. When handcrafted, throwback cocktails first migrated west and south from New York and San Fran, they landed here, amid velvet booths and well-dressed, mustachioed bartenders. (☎310-854-1300; www.therogerroom.com; 370 N La Cienega Blvd; ⏰6pm-2am Mon-Fri, from 7pm Sat, from 8pm Sun)

Beverly Hills Juice Club   JUICE BAR

21 Map p56, E4

This 1975 hippie classic – the first on the LA health-food, raw-power band-

wagon – started out on Sunset when Tom Waits and Rickie Lee Jones used to stumble in between shows. It still attracts an in-the-know crowd craving wheatgrass shots and banana-manna shakes. Get yours with a shot of algae. No, seriously. (☎323-655-8300; www.beverlyhillsjuice.com; 8382 Beverly Blvd; ⏰7am-6pm Mon-Fri, from 9am Sat)

Entertainment

Largo at the Coronet   LIVE MUSIC, PERFORMING ARTS

22 ⭐ Map p56, D4

Ever since its early days on Fairfax Ave, Largo has been progenitor of high-minded pop culture (it nurtured Zach Galifianakis to stardom). Now part of the Coronet Theatre complex, it features edgy comedy, such as Sarah Silverman and Nick Offerman, and nourishing night music such as the Preservation Hall Jazz Band. (☎310-855-0530; www.largo-la.com; 366 N La Cienega Blvd)

Roxy Theatre   LIVE MUSIC

23 ⭐ Map p56, C2

A Sunset fixture since 1973, the Roxy has presented everyone from Miles Davis to David Bowie to Jane's Addiction, and still occasionally manages to book music that matters today. It's a small venue, so you'll be up close and personal with the bands. (www.theroxy.com; 9009 W Sunset Blvd)

Troubadour
LIVE MUSIC

24 ⭐ Map p56, C3

This celebrated 1957 rock hall launched 1000 careers, including those of James Taylor and Tom Waits, and was central to John Lennon's 'Lost Weekend in 1973'. It's still a great spot for catching tomorrow's headliners and appeals to beer-drinking music aficionados who keep attitude to a minimum. Come early to snag a seat on the balcony. No age limit. (www.troubadour.com; 9081 Santa Monica Blvd)

Vibrato Grill Bar
JAZZ

25 ⭐ Map p56, A3

You can thank Grammy Award–winning jazz legend Herb Alpert for the standout acoustics here. After all, he designed this elegant, romantic spot. A restaurant and jazz club in one, it serves up six nights of stellar acts, from Cali standouts such as Freddie Ravel and the Joshua White Trio, to international guests such as Maria Elena Infantino. Reservations (and smart outfits) are highly recommended. (☏310-474-9400; www.vibratogrilljazz.com; 2930 Beverly Glen Cir; ☺5-10pm Tue-Thu & Sun, to 11pm Fri & Sat)

Whisky-a-Go-Go
LIVE MUSIC

26 ⭐ Map p56, C2

Like other aging Sunset Strip venues, the Whisky coasts more on its legend status than current relevance. Yup, this was where the Doors were the house band and go-go dancing was invented back in the '60s. These days the stage usually belongs to long-shot hard rockers. (☏310-652-4202; www.whiskyagogo.com; 8901 W Sunset Blvd)

Nuart Theatre
CINEMA

27 ⭐ Map p56, A5

This dank, but still hip, art and revival house presents the best in offbeat and cult flicks, including a highly interactive screening of *The Rocky Horror Picture Show* ($12) supported by an

 Top Tip

Yuk it Up

Some of America's leading comics got their feet wet right here at WeHo's comedy clubs. The **Comedy Store** (☏323-650-6268; www.thecomedystore.com; 8433 W Sunset Blvd) has been a thing since it brought in hot young comics such as Robin Williams and David Letterman. The Marx Brothers kept offices at the **Laugh Factory** (☏323-656-1336; www.laughfactory.com; 8001 W Sunset Blvd) and it still gets some big names. **The Groundlings** (☏323-934-4747; www.groundlings.com; 7307 Melrose Ave; tickets $10-20) improv school and company launched Will Ferrell, Maya Rudolph and other top talent, while the **Improv** (www.improv.com; 8162 Melrose Ave; prices vary; ☺show times vary) launched countless stand-ups like Jerry Seinfeld and Ellen DeGeneres and still gigs in up-and-comers.

outrageous live cast at midnight on Saturdays. Bring glow sticks and toilet paper. (☑310-473-8530; www.landmark theaters.com; 11272 Santa Monica Blvd; adult/senior & child $11/9)

Shopping

Book Soup   BOOKS

28 Map p56, C2

A bibliophile's indie gem, sprawling and packed with entertainment, travel, feminist and queer studies,

---

> ### Local Life
> ### All in All it's Just a... Nother Day at the Mall
> If Rodeo Dr or Melrose Ave aren't your speed, two giant malls attract tons of locals. Faux Italian palazzo **Grove** (www.thegrovela.com; 189 The Grove Dr; ℙ🅿; 🚌MTA lines 16, 17, 780 to Wilshire & Fairfax) is one of LA's most popular shopping destinations, with 40 name-brand stores, a fountain and a trolley rolling down the middle. The eight-story, monolithic **Beverly Center** (☑310-854-0070; www.beverlycenter.com; 8500 Beverly Blvd; ⊙10am-9pm Mon-Fri, to 8pm Sat, to 6pm Sun), anchored by Bloomingdale's and Macy's department stores and home to some 100 other national and international brands, is undergoing a $500-million facelift and interior redesign, scheduled for completion by late 2018 – shops remain open for the duration.

---

eclectic and LA-based fiction, with appearances by big-name authors. (☑310-659-3110; www.booksoup.com; 8818 W Sunset Blvd; ⊙9am-10pm Mon-Sat, to 7pm Sun)

Mystery Pier Books   BOOKS

29 Map p56, C2

An intimate, hidden-away courtyard shop that specializes in selling signed shooting scripts from past blockbusters and first editions from Shakespeare (from 1734; $2500 to $4000), Salinger ($21,000) and JK Rowling ($30,000 and up). (www.mysterypier books.com; 8826 W Sunset Blvd; ⊙11am-7pm Mon-Sat, noon-5pm Sun)

Meltdown Comics & Collectibles   COLLECTIBLES

30 Map p56, G1

LA's coolest comic store proudly lets its geek flag fly, with indie and mainstream comic books, from Japanese manga to graphic novels, and all the relevant pop-cool merch you can shake a lightsaber at. It also stages a changing lineup of events, from lectures to comedy to trivia; visit the Nerdmelt tab on the website for deets (www.meltcomics.com; 7522 Sunset Blvd; ⊙11am-9pm Thu-Tue, 10am-10pm Wed; 🐾)

Melrose Avenue   FASHION

31 Map p56, G3

A popular shopping strip as famous for its epic people-watching as it is for its consumer fruits. You'll see hair

Book Soup

and people) of all shades and styles, and everything from Gothic jewels to custom sneakers to medical marijuana to stuffed porcupines available for a price. The strip is located between Fairfax and La Brea Aves.

Barneys New York DEPARTMENT STORE

32 🔒 Map p56, A5

The Beverly Hills branch of New York's most fashion-forward department store delivers four floors of sharply curated collections for women and men. Expect interesting pieces from luxe Euro brands such as Givenchy and Gucci, as well as unique pieces from homegrown labels like 3.1 Philip Lim and Warm.

Prices are steep, so keep an eye out for one of its end-of-season sales. Once spent, refuel at the notable 5th-floor **restaurant** (☏310-777-5877; www.barneys. com/store/R-store-902; mains $22-32; ⌚11am-7pm Mon-Sat, 11:30am-6:30pm Sun). (☏310-276-4400; www.barneys.com; 9570 Wilshire Blvd; ⌚10am-7pm Mon-Wed, Fri & Sat, to 8pm Thu, 11am-6pm Sun; 📶)

Top Sights
Getty Center

Getting There

🚗 The Getty Center is best accessed from the I-405, exit Getty Center Dr. Parking is $15.

🚌 You can take the bus (Metro 734, 234), which stops at the main gate.

In its billion-dollar, in-the-clouds perch, high above the city grit and grime, the Getty Center presents triple delights: a stellar art collection (everything from medieval triptychs to baroque sculpture and impressionist brushstrokes), Richard Meier's cutting-edge architecture and the visual splendor of seasonally changing gardens. On clear days, add in breathtaking views of the city and ocean.

Richard Meier's Architecture

As famous for its built form as it is for its art, the Getty Center was designed by Pritzker Prize–winning architect Richard Meier. Cubic forms and horizontal lines define the modernist 4-building complex, completed in 1997.

It's clad in 16,000 tons of beige travertine marble sourced from the same Italian quarry used to construct Rome's ancient Colosseum. Look closely and you'll see ancient, fossilized shells, fish and foliage.

Central Garden

More than a few visitors spend more time outside the museum's hallowed halls than inside, thanks to the magnificent, Robert Irwin–designed central garden. The 134,000-sq-ft design includes a stream that winds through and past 500-plus plant varieties that twist into a labyrinthine swirl.

Permanent Collection

Although not everyone is captivated by the Getty's collection of European art, which spans the 17th to 20th centuries, there are some gems. Pieces from the baroque period can be found in the east pavilion, the west pavilion features neoclassical and Romantic sculpture and decorative arts, while the north pavilion is stuffed with medieval and Renaissance pieces. Must-sees include Van Gogh's *Irises*, Monet's *Wheatstacks*, Rembrandt's *The Abduction of Europa* and Titian's *Venus and Adonis*.

Special Exhibits

If old Euro art isn't your jam, special exhibits almost always contain something edgy and contemporary, like mind-bending installations and unique photography or multimedia exhibits.

📞 310-440-7300

www.getty.edu

1200 Getty Center Dr

admission free

🕙 10am-5:30pm Tue-Fri & Sun, to 9pm Sat

☑ Top Tips

▶ Children can take a Family Tour, visit the interactive Family Room, borrow a kid-oriented audioguide or browse the special kid bookstore.

▶ The **Saturdays Off the 405** (www.getty.edu; Getty Center; 🕙 6-9pm Sat May-Sep) performance serves up some tremendous progressive pop and world-music acts in the Getty courtyard.

✕ Take a Break

Before or after the Getty, detour to **Sawtelle Japantown** a few miles away. **Tsujita LA** (📞 310-231-7373; http://tsujita-la.com; 2057 Sawtelle Blvd; ramen $10-15; 🕙 11am-1:30am) and **Yakitoriya** (📞 310-479-5400; 11301 W Olympic Blvd; dishes $2.50-27; 🕙 6-10:30pm Wed-Mon) are great options.

Explore

Miracle Mile & Mid-City

Mid-City encompasses the Miracle Mile – home to some of the best museums in the west – the Orthodox-Jewish-meets-hipster Fairfax district and the legendary rock, punk and vintage shopping strip of Melrose Ave.

The Sights in a Day

☼ Enjoy pastry and coffee at **Republique** (p79), then hit **LACMA** (p74) to explore the permanent collections, rotating exhibitions and installations. If the kids get bored, stroll them over to the gooey **La Brea Tar Pits** (p72), or hightail across the street to the **Petersen Automotive Museum** (p78).

☼ Grown-ups should grab a New American lunch at **Ray's** (p81). Grown-ups with kids should head up to the **Grove** (p66) and the **Original Farmers Market** (p82) for sustenance. Hipsters will appreciate the eco-conscious style of **Reformation** (p84) on La Brea. Skate punks and hip-hop freaks should make way to the Fairfax Ave showrooms.

☾ At dinner, seafood lovers enjoy **Son of a Gun** (p60), while carnivores descend on **Animal** (p80). Grab craft tequila at **El Carmen** (p82), then watch a show at **El Rey** (p83) or **Mint** (p84).

◉ Top Sights

La Brea Tar Pits & Museum (p72)

LACMA (p74)

🖤 Best of Los Angeles

Eating

Canter's (p81)

Crossroads (p81)

Museums

LACMA (p74)

Petersen Automotive Museum (p78)

Wall Project (p79)

Drinking

El Carmen (p82)

Getting There

🚌 **Bus** Use city buses such as Metro lines 10 (along Melrose Ave), 14 (along Beverly Blvd) and 20 and 720 (along Wilshire Blvd).

Top Sights
La Brea Tar Pits & Museum

Mammoths, saber-toothed cats and dire wolves used to roam LA's savannah in prehistoric times. We know this because of an archaeological trove of skulls and bones unearthed here at the La Brea Tar Pits, one of the world's most fecund and famous fossil sites. A museum has been built here, where generations of young dino-hunters have come to seek out fossils and learn about paleontology from docents and demonstrations in on-site labs.

👁 Map p76, E4

www.tarpits.org

5801 Wilshire Blvd, Mid-City

adult/student & senior/child $12/9/5, 1st Tue of month Sep-Jun free

🕑9:30am-5pm

P 🚻

Project 23

During the construction of LACMA's underground parking complex, 16 new fossil deposits were discovered, including a nearly complete skeleton of an adult mammoth. Paleontologists at the museum helped preserve the fossilized bones, creating 23 fossil blocks. In 2008 excavation began and the fossils are now on public view, while excavators work seven days a week with hand tools such as dental picks, chisels, hammers and brushes to preserve and clean their bounty. This project will keep the lab busy for years.

Pit 91

Located just west of the museum is the Pit 91 excavation site; before Project 23, this was the only active excavation site at Rancho La Brea during the past 40 years. Discovered during the 1913–15 excavations it was decided that this large cluster of fossils would be left in the tar as a 'showpiece'. Unfortunately, the site suffered repeated cave-ins and floods, and it was ultimately abandoned, with thousands of fossils still awaiting excavation. In the summer of 2014, paleontologists began digging back in!

Museum Collections

While all the giddy paleontologists and curious visitors converge around Pit 91 and Project 23, don't forget that within the museum itself are 3.5 million fossil specimens of over 10,000 individuals representing 600-plus species of prehistoric mammals (90% of which were carnivores), birds (one of the largest collections of its kind in the world), flora, invertebrates, fish, amphibians and reptiles.

☑ **Top Tips**

▶ Inside the Tar Pits' 3-D cinema, the 25-minute film *Titans of the Ice Age* screens 10am to 4pm daily (extra charge adult/child $4/3).

▶ *La* is Spanish for 'the' and *brea* is Spanish for 'tar,' so 'the La Brea Tar Pits' literally means 'the the Tar Tar Pits'.

✗ Take a Break

One of the first market cafes in the LA area, Joan's on Third (p61) is still one of the best. The coffee and pastries are absurdly good, and the deli churns out tasty gourmet sandwiches and salads. It's a great place to pick up provisions for a day at the beach or a night at the Hollywood Bowl.

Top Sights
Los Angeles County Museum of Art (LACMA)

The depth and wealth of the collection at the largest museum in the western US is stunning. LACMA holds all the major players – Rembrandt, Cézanne, Magritte, Mary Cassatt, Ansel Adams – plus millennia worth of Chinese, Japanese, pre-Columbian and ancient Greek, Roman and Egyptian sculpture. Between 2008 and 2010, architect Renzo Piano designed two of the newer gallery buildings on the western side of the campus.

👁 Map p76, E4

📞 323-857-6000

www.lacma.org

5905 Wilshire Blvd

adult/child $15/free

🕐 11am-5pm Mon, Tue & Thu, to 8pm Fri, 10am-7pm Sat & Sun

Japanese Art Pavilion

Pieces in this oh-so-Zen pavilion range in origin from 3000 BC to the 21st century. Here are Buddhist and Shinto sculpture, ancient ceramics and lacquerware, textiles and armor, and the epic Kasamatsu Shiro woodblock print, *Cherry Blossoms at Toshogu Shrine.*

Art Collections

Recent acquisitions include massive outdoor installations such as Chris Burden's *Urban Light* (a surreal selfie backdrop of hundreds of vintage LA streetlamps) and Michael Heizer's *Levitated Mass,* a surprisingly inspirational 340-ton boulder perched over a walkway.

Renovations

The rest of the campus is now about to see a major makeover, courtesy of Swiss architect Peter Zumthor. Renovation plans call for most of the current mid-century pavilions (so in need of work as to be untenable) to be razed and airy, cantilevered galleries to replace them, straddling Wilshire Blvd. The redesign is scheduled for completion in 2023. Until then, several of the galleries will remain open (thankfully the jewel-box Pavilion for Japanese Art is staying put) and parts of the collection will be exhibited elsewhere around LA.

Check the website for construction schedules and to learn which galleries will remain open during the renovation.

☑ Top Tips

▶ Short on cash? Visit on the second Tuesday of the month and you can have access to all collections and exhibits for free.

▶ The **Academy Museum**, future home of the museum of the Oscars, is scheduled to open adjacent to LACMA in 2019.

▶ Jazz fans should stick around on Friday nights for **Jazz at LACMA** (admission free; ⊘6pm Fri).

✖ Take a Break

Once you pay the relatively steep admission, odds are you won't want to stray too far from campus when your stomach grumbles. Just step over to Ray's (p81) for New American cuisine, or find a cheap and cheerful food truck across the street.

For reviews see

👁	Top Sights	p72
◉	Sights	p78
✕	Eating	p79
🍷	Drinking	p82
★	Entertainment	p83
🛍	Shopping	p84

Melrose Pl

25 🔒

Melrose Ave

13 ✕

24

29 🔒

19 🛍

N Fairfax Ave

Clinton St

N Sweetzer Ave

N Laurel Ave

N Edinburgh Ave

N Hayworth Ave

N Crescent Heights Blvd

Rosewood Ave

BEVERLY CENTER DISTRICT

9 ✕

14 ✕

Oakwood Ave

S La Jolla Ave

Beverly Blvd

N La Cienega Blvd

Beverly Blvd

W 1st St

S Edinburgh Ave

S Hayworth Ave

Far
Mar

W 3rd St

16 🍷

Gr
15

S Fairfax Ave

Burton Way

Colgate Ave

Clifton Way

S Orlando Ave

Colgate Ave

S Crescent Heights Blvd

S Sweetzer Ave

S La Jolla Ave

MID-CITY

Wilshire Blvd

Zimmer Children's Museum
◉ 5

Wilshire Blvd

S Corning St

S La Cienega Blvd

La Cienega Park

S San Vicente Blvd

Petersen Automotive Museum ◉ 1

S Orange Grove Ave

S Ogden Dr

W Olympic Blvd

22 ★

W Olympic Blvd

E **F** **G** **H**

Melrose Ave

28

26

N 0
0
1 km
0.5 miles

18

MELROSE/
LA BREA

12

Clinton St

N Genesee Ave
N Spaulding Ave
N Stanley Ave
N Curson Ave
N Sierra Bonita Ave
N Gardner St
N Vista St
N Martel Ave
N Fuller Ave
N Poinsettia Pl
N Alta Vista Blvd
N Formosa Ave
N Detroit St
N La Brea Ave
N Sycamore Ave
N Highland Ave
N Las Palmas Ave

Oakwood Ave

FAIRFAX
DISTRICT

1

2

Beverly Blvd

HANCOCK
PARK

CBS Television
City

Pan
Pacific
Park

MID-CITY

W 1st St

S Orange Dr
S Mansfield Ave
S Citrus Ave
N Highland Ave
N Mc Cadden Pl
S Las Palmas Ave

31

23

The Grove Dr
S Gardner St
S Vista St
S Martel Ave
S Fuller Ave
S Poinsettia Pl
S Alta Vista Blvd
S Formosa Ave

W 2nd St

3

W 3rd St

S Alta Vista Blvd
S La Brea Ave
S Sycamore Ave
S McCadden Pl

W 4th St

4

os Angeles County
Museum
f Art

W 6th St

La Brea Tar
Pits & Museum

MIRACLE
MILE

W 6th St

7

Wilshire Blvd

6
ll
ject

2
Craft &
Folk Art
Museum

21

Ace Gallery

27

4
8

S Ridgeley Dr
S Dunsmuir Ave
S Cochran Ave
S Cloverdale Ave
S Detroit St
S Orange Dr
S Mansfield Ave
S Citrus Ave

ele Ave
S Stanley Ave
S Curson Ave

5

Sights

Petersen Automotive Museum
MUSEUM

1 Map p76, D5

A four-story ode to the auto, the Petersen Automotive Museum is a treat even for those who can't tell a piston from a carburetor. A headlights-to-brake-lights futuristic makeover (by Kohn Pedersen Fox) in late 2015 left it fairly gleaming from the outside; the exterior is undulating bands of stainless steel on a hot-rod-red background. The once-dowdy inside is now equally gripping, with floors themed for the history, industry and artistry of motorized transportation. (☎323-930-2277; www.petersen.org; 6060 Wilshire Blvd; adult/senior & student/child $15/12/7; ⏰10am-6pm; P ♿; ☒Metro lines 20, 217, 720, 780 to Wilshire & Fairfax)

Craft & Folk Art Museum
MUSEUM

2 ◉ Map p76, E5

This well-respected, intimate, three-story museum features an eclectic mix of world-renowned and local, up-and-coming artists in the folk and craft art worlds. The museum's goal is to straddle the lines between the contemporary-art, socio-political movements and craft media you don't always see: fiber arts, metal working, book-binding and more. Exhibits change every few months, so check for closing dates and for family-oriented hands-on workshops, usually held on Sundays. (☎323-937-4230; www.cafam.org; 5814 Wilshire Blvd; adult/student & senior/under 12yr $7/5/free, 1st Thu of month free 6:30-9:30pm; ⏰11am-5pm Tue-Fri, to 6pm Sat & Sun; ♿; ☒MTA line 20 to Wilshire & Curson)

CBS Television City
STUDIO

3 ◉ Map p76, E2

North of the Farmers Market (p82) is CBS, where game shows, talk shows, soap operas and other programs are taped, often before a live audience, including the *Late Late Show with James Corden, Real Time with Bill Maher* and the perennially popular *The Price Is Right* game show. Check online for tickets. (www.cbs.com; 7800 Beverly Blvd)

Ace Gallery
GALLERY

4 ◉ Map p76, F5

This amazing gallery sprawls an entire floor of the Desmond Building (c 1927). The art is all modern-edged, including minimalist canvases, strobing video installations, plexiglass orbs and rusted coils of steel. Over they years it's exhibited pretty much every big name, and the current exhibits from a worldwide stable of artists change between weekly and six monthly. (☎323-935-4411; www.acegallery.net; 5514 Wilshire Blvd, 2nd fl; admission free; ⏰10am-6pm Tue-Sat)

Zimmer Children's Museum
MUSEUM

5 ◉ Map p76, C4

In the Jewish Federation Center, this charming museum brims with interactive exhibits that gently teach

CBS Television City

kids about tolerance, generosity and community spirit. Kids 'fly' to exotic lands, become ambulance drivers, work the newsroom and take other fun journeys. Check the calendar for a roster of singalongs and workshops. (☎323-761-8984; www.zimmermuseum. org; 6505 Wilshire Blvd, Suite 100; admission $7.50; ☺10am-5pm Mon-Thu, to 4pm Fri, 12:30-4:30pm Sun; P♿; 🚍Metro line 20 to Wilshire & La Jolla)

Wall Project PUBLIC ART

6 ◉ Map p76, E5

Ten slabs of the old Berlin Wall, augmented by well-known street artists, are on display on the lawn of a Wilshire high-rise across the street from LACMA as part of the global Wall Project, curated by the fabulous Wende Museum (p87) in Culver City. It's the largest stretch of the wall outside of Germany – LA and Berlin are sister cities. (www.wendemuseum. org/collections/berlin-wall-segments; 5900 Wilshire Blvd; admission free)

Eating

Republique BISTRO $$$

7 ✖ Map p76, G4

A design gem with the gourmet ambition to match. The old interior of LA's dearly departed Campanile is still an atrium restaurant with stone arches, a brightly lit front end scattered with butcher-block tables, and a marble bar peering into an open kitchen. There are tables in the darker, oakier backroom too. (📞310-362-6115; www.republiquela.com; 624 S La Brea Ave; mains lunch $11-19, dinner $14-56; 🕐8am-4pm daily, 5:30-10pm Sun-Thu, to 11pm Fri & Sat; P🚻; 🚍MTA line 20, 720)

Yuko Kitchen
JAPANESE $

 Map p76, F5

This brightly painted, artsy-adorable Japanese-fusion cafe (enter just south of Wilshire Blvd) serves sashimi salads, udon, rice bowls piled with miso-flavored ground beef, grilled tofu, spicy salmon and smelt eggs, albacore sashimi and generous plate lunches. 'Bowl-litos' are Japanese-style burritos, wrapped in nori seaweed. It also makes terrific desserts. Staff are lovely and there's seating inside and out. (📞323-933-4020; www.yukokitchen.com; 5484 Wilshire Blvd; mains $9-12; 🕐11am-9:30pm Mon-Sat; ❄)

Animal
GRILL $$$

 Map p76, D2

Carnivorous foodies pray at the altar of Animal, the restaurant that put food bros Jon Shook and Vinny Dotolo on the map. Begin with chicken-liver toast or spicy beef tendons (with charred-onion pho dip) then get the smoked turkey leg with celery root, apple and white barbecue sauce, or foie gras loco moco. Simultaneously serious and playful.

It's on the traditionally Jewish strip of Fairfax Ave, yet – irony of ironies – virtually nothing on the menu is kosher. (📞323-782-9225; www.animalrestaurant.com; 435 N Fairfax Ave; dishes $6-39; 🕐6-10pm Mon-Thu, to 11pm Fri, 10:30am-2:30pm & 6-11pm Sat, 10:30am-2:30pm & 6-10pm Sun)

Lotería! Grill
MEXICAN $

 Map p76, D3

This unpretentious yet gourmet taco stand in the Original Farmers Market (p82) is often credited with starting LA's boom in authentic, regional Mexican cooking. It's known for preps such as *cochinita pibil* (achiote and citrus-marinated pork), chicken *tinga* (stewed with chipotle peppers and

---

Understand
Hancock Park

There's nothing quite like the old-money mansions flanking the tree-lined streets of Hancock Park, a genteel neighborhood roughly bounded by Highland, Rossmore and Melrose Aves and Wilshire Blvd. In the 1920s, LA's leading families, including the Dohenys and Chandlers, hired famous architects to build their pads, and celebrities such as Damon Wayans, Melanie Griffith, Jason Alexander and Manny Pacquiao have lived here. It's a lovely area for a stroll or a drive, especially around Christmas when houses sparkle.

chorizo) and nopalito cactus salad. Try all the varieties on minitacos in a Probaditas plate. (☎323-930-2211; www. loteriagrill.com; 6333 W 3rd St, Original Farmers Market; tacos & burritos $3.25-12, combo plates $13-19; ⊙9am-9pm Mon-Thu, to 10pm Fri & Sat, to 8pm Sun; P ♿)

Ray's

MODERN AMERICAN $$$

 11 Map p76, E4

Seldom does a restaurant blessed with as golden a location as this one – on the plaza of LACMA (p74) – live up to the address. Ray's does. Menus change seasonally and often daily with farm-to-table fresh ingredients – some grown in the restaurant's own garden. You can expect some form of burrata, kale salad and pizzas to be on the menu. (☎323-857-6180; www.raysandstark bar.com; Los Angeles County Museum of Art, 5905 Wilshire Blvd; mains $17-36; ⊙11:30am-8pm Mon-Tue & Thu, to 10pm Fri, 10am-8pm Sat & Sun; P ; ☒MTA 20)

Osteria & Pizzeria Mozza

ITALIAN $$$

 12 Map p76, H1

Osteria Mozza crafts fine cuisine from market-fresh, seasonal ingredients, but being a Mario Batali joint, you can expect adventure – think squid-ink chitarra freddi with Dungeness crab, sea urchin and jalapeño – and consistent excellence. Reservations are recommended. Next door, Pizzeria Mozza is more laid-back and cheaper, its gorgeous thin-crust pies topped with combos such as squash blossoms,

tomato and creamy burrata. (☎osteria 323-297-0100, pizzeria 323-297-0101; http:// la.osteriamozza.com; pizzas $11-25, osteria mains $29-38; ⊙pizzeria noon-midnight, osteria 5:30-11pm Mon-Fri, 5-11pm Sat, 5-10pm Sun; P)

Crossroads

VEGAN $$

 13 Map p76, C1

Tal Ronnen didn't get to be a celebrity chef (Oprah, Ellen) by serving ordinary vegan fare. Instead, seasonal creations include 'crab cakes' made from hearts of palm, artichoke 'oysters,' and porcini-crusted eggplant, alongside pizzas and pastas incorporating innovative 'cheeses' made from nuts. Leave the Birkenstocks at home; this place is sophisticated, with full bar and cool cocktails. (☎323-782-9245; www.crossroadskitchen.com; 8284 Melrose Ave; brunch mains $7-14, dinner mains $12-22; ⊙10am-2pm daily, 5-10pm Sun-Thu, to midnight Fri & Sat; ☒)

Canter's

DELI $$

 14 Map p76, D2

As old-school delis go, Canter's is hard to beat. A fixture in the traditionally Jewish Fairfax district since 1931, it serves up the requisite pastrami, corned beef and matzo-ball soup with a side of sass by seen-it-all waitresses, in a rangy room with deli and bakery counters up front.

The adjacent Kibitz Room is part-restaurant, part-dive-bar, and has been visited over the decades by rockers from Frank Zappa to Joni

Mitchell, Guns 'n' Roses and Jakob Dylan. There are still performances most nights. Who knows? You might catch tomorrow's big star. (323-651-2030; www.cantersdeli.com; 419 N Fairfax Ave; ⏱24hr; Ⓟ)

Original Farmers Market

MARKET $

15 Map p76, D3

The Farmers Market is a great spot for a casual meal any time of day, especially if the rug rats are tagging along. There are lots of options here, from gumbo and diner food to Singapore-style noodles and tacos, sit-down or takeout. Before or afterwards, go check out the Grove (p66), next door. (📞323-933-9211; www.farmersmarketla.com; 6333 W 3rd St; mains $6-12; ⏱9am-9pm Mon-Fri, to 8pm Sat, 10am-7pm Sun; Ⓟ👶)

Drinking

El Carmen

BAR

16 🍷 Map p76, C3

A pair of mounted bull heads and *lucha libre* (Mexican wrestling) masks create an over-the-top, 'Tijuana North' look and pull in an industry-heavy crowd at LA's ultimate tequila tavern (over 300 to choose from). If you don't know an *añejo* from a *reposado,* do a tasting and find out (from $25), or just get a perfect tequila cocktail.

There's a short but mighty menu of tamales, tacos, enchiladas and sides.

(📞323-852-1552; www.elcarmenla.com; 8138 W 3rd St; ⏱5pm-2am)

Stark Bar

BAR

17 🍷 Map p76, E4

The closest you can get to LACMA's *Urban Light* with a drink in your hand, this bar on the museum's plaza specializes in draft cocktails and frozen ones like the Hemingway daiquiri, and uses spirits from small-batch distillers. The water sommelier can match bottled water to the bites you get from Ray's (p81) next door. (Los Angeles County Museum of Art, 5905 Wilshire Blvd)

Cat & Fiddle

PUB

18 🍷 Map p76, H1

In new Hollywood digs, this much-loved British pub will have you pining for Old Blighty with its mix of UK ales (think Newcastle Brown Ale and Old Speckled Hen) and salt-of-the-earth atmosphere. And did we mention the lovely patio? (www.thecatandfiddle.com; 742 N Highland Ave; ⏱11:30am-1am Mon-Fri, from 10am Sat & Sun; 📶)

Crumbs & Whiskers

CAT CAFE

19 🍷 Map p76, D1

Humans commune with kitties at LA's first cat cafe. The spare, stylish black-box storefront is kitted out with fluffy futons and climbing shelves, and humans can observe and gently touch felines while drinking coffee and tea. Resident cats were rescued from high-

Crepe shop, Original Farmers Market

kill shelters and are up for adoption, but here you're in their environment, not the other way around. (☎323-879-9389; www.crumbsandwhiskers.com; 7924 Melrose Ave; 75min visit weekdays/weekends $22/25; ⊙11am-7:45pm Thu-Tue; 🖼)

Paramount Coffee Project CAFE

20 Map p76, D2

Aussie-run PCP gets its coffee from Sydney's famed Reuben Hills coffee roaster, and it makes its own almond milk and macadamia milk. Food includes breakfast and all-day sandwiches, avocado toast, noodles and salads. Sit in the long, narrow, modernist room or order to-go from the window. (☎323-746-5480; www.pcpfx.

com; 456 N Fairfax Ave; ⊙7am-5pm Mon-Sat, from 8am Sun)

Entertainment

El Rey   LIVE MUSIC

21 ⭐ Map p76, F5

A 1931 art deco dance hall decked out in red velvet and chandeliers and flaunting an awesome sound system and excellent sightlines. Although it can hold nearly 800 people, it feels more intimate. It brings in everything from cover bands to pretty big names, so check the calendar. (www.theelrey.com; 5515 Wilshire Blvd; cover varies)

Local Life

Larchmont Avenue

Who dropped Mayberry in the middle of Los Angeles? With its stroller-friendly coffee shops, locally owned boutiques and low-key patios, Larchmont is an oasis of square normality bordering a desert of Hollywood hipness.

Mint   CONCERT VENUE

22 ⭐ Map p76, B5

Built in 1937, Mint is an intimate, historic venue. Legends such as Ray Charles and Stevie Wonder played here on the way up, and axe-man Ben Harper got his start here, too. Expect a packed slate of terrific jazz, blues and rock shows, sensational sound, and you'll never be more than 30ft from the performance stage. (www.themintla.com; 6010 W Pico Blvd; cover $5-25)

Pacific Theatres at the Grove   CINEMA

23 ⭐ Map p76, E3

A fancy all-stadium, 14-screen multiplex with comfy reclining seats, wall-to-wall screens and superb sound. The Monday Morning Mommy Movies series (11am) gives the diaper-bag brigade a chance to catch a flick with their tots, but without hostile stares from nonbreeders. (www.pacifictheatres.com; 189 The Grove Dr; adult/senior & children $14.25/11.25; ♿)

Shopping

Fred Segal   FASHION & ACCESSORIES

24 🔒 Map p76, C1

Celebs and beautiful people circle for the very latest from Babakul, Aviator Nation and Robbi & Nikki at this warren of high-end boutiques under one impossibly chic but slightly snooty roof. The only time you'll see bargains (sort of) is during the two-week blowout sale in September. (☎ 323-651-4129; www.fredsegal.com; 8100 Melrose Ave; ⏱10am-7pm Mon-Sat, noon-6pm Sun)

Reformation   FASHION & ACCESSORIES

25 🔒 Map p76, C1

Here's classic, retro-inspired, fashionable women's wear that's eco-conscious without the granola. It does it by using pre-existing materials, which means no additional dyeing of fabrics and half the water use of other fashion brands, and with an eye toward minimizing waste from sourcing to production, sales and even recycling. Everything is made locally. (www.thereformation.com; 8253 Melrose Ave; ⏱11am-7pm Mon-Sat, to 6pm Sun)

Wasteland   VINTAGE

26 🔒 Map p76, F1

Large, popular and rather-polished vintage boutique with racks packed with skirts and tops, fur-collared jackets and Pendleton wool shirts. (www.shopwasteland.com; 7428 Melrose Ave; ⏱11am-8pm Mon-Sat, from noon Sun)

Whimsic Alley

GIFTS & SOUVENIRS

27 Map p76, F5

Indulge your passion for British sci-fi, fantasy and drama at this unusual outfitter styled after Diagon Alley of *Harry Potter* fame. Whimsic Alley purveys wands, capes and Hogwarts sweaters, *Game of Thrones* memorabilia, *Sherlock Holmes*– and *Dr Who*–inspired costumes and souvenirs and even a *Downton Abbey* section. Check out the holograms lining the hallway – blimey! (☎310-453-2370; www.whimsic alley.com; 5464 Wilshire Blvd; ⏱11am-6pm Mon-Fri, from 10am Sat & Sun; 🚻)

ASH

FASHION & ACCESSORIES

28 Map p76, E1

This thumping shop sells street wear and designer wear mostly for men, with brands such as Tokyo's Iro-ichi (band jackets of embroidered denim) and Black Pyramid (singer Chris Brown's clothing line). But we love LA designer Rik Villa's amazing repurposing of old duffel bags, deconstructed jeans and more to create cool, one-of-a-kind jackets. (A Sexy Habit; ☎323-944-0529; 7614½ Melrose Ave; ⏱noon-8pm)

Great Frog

JEWELRY

29 Map p76, D1

A sterling-silver jewelry company known for its skulls, Great Frog started in London, has a shop in NYC and this is its latest offering. It casts in gold as well, and sells leather jackets. We loved the vintage motorcycle engines in the jewelry case and the stunning 1941 Indian in the window. (☎323-879-9100; www.thegreatfroglondon.com; 7955 Melrose Ave; ⏱11am-7pm Mon-Sat, noon-6pm Sun)

Record Collector

MUSIC

30 Map p76, E1

If you dig vinyl – specifically jazz and classical on vinyl – you must check out this record trader. It's stuffed floor to ceiling and staffed with a shopkeeper who would love to help you hunt down the gems, but it's best to have something particular in mind – then they can really help you. They've been doing it since 1974. (☎323-655-6653; 7809 Melrose Ave; ⏱10am-5pm daily)

American Girl Place

DOLLS

31 Map p76, E3

Little girls go gaga for this make-believe toy land where they can take their plastic friends to lunch or afternoon tea at the cafe or a revue-style show, get photographed for a mock *American Girls* magazine cover at the photo studio, or give them a makeover in the doll hair salon. (www.americangirl.com; 189 The Grove Dr, Grove Mall; ⏱10am-7pm Mon-Thu, to 9pm Fri & Sat, to 6pm Sun; 🚻)

Local Life
Gallery Hopping in Culver City

Getting There

🚗 Culver City is accessible via Robertson Blvd from Mid-City and from Washington Blvd in Venice.

🚆 The Culver City line serves areas in the city, Santa Monica, Venice and West LA.

A decade ago Culver City bloomed from its bland, semisuburban studio-town roots into a stylish yet unpretentious destination for fans of art, culture and food, and it happened organically. Then the 2008 recession hit and Culver City buckled. But the roots of groovy stayed alive, and this 'hood has come back stronger than ever.

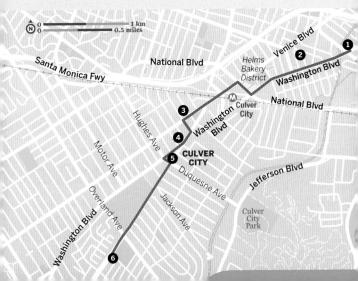

❶ Gallery Gazing

A major US art player and juggernaut of the Culver City arts district, **Blum & Poe** (📞310-836-2062; www.blumandpoe. com; 2727 S La Cienega Blvd; 🕙10am-6pm Tue-Sat) reps international stars Takashi Murakami, Sam Durant and Sharon Lockhart.

❷ Roaming the District

The Helms complex marks the beginning of Culver City's vital **Arts District** (https://culvercityartsdistrict.com; La Cienega Blvd), which runs east along Washington to La Cienega and up one block to Venice Blvd.

❸ Something Strange

Arguably LA's most intriguing exhibition space, the **Museum of Jurassic Technology** (MJT; 📞310-836-6131; www. mjt.org; 9341 Venice Blvd; suggested donation adult/student & senior/under 13yr $8/5/free; 🕙2-8pm Thu, noon-6pm Fri-Sun) has nothing to do with dinosaurs and even less with technology. Instead, you'll find madness nibbling at your synapses as you try to read meaning into mind-bending displays about Cameroonian stink ants and microscopic pope sculpture.

❹ Taste of the Town

There's no shortage of creative kitchens in Culver. **Akasha** (📞310-845-1700; www. akasharestaurant.com; 9543 Culver Blvd; dinner mains $15-30, cafe dishes $4-13.50; 🕙restaurant 11:30am-2:30pm & 5:30-9:30pm Mon-Thu, to 10:30pm Fri, 10:30am-2:30pm & 5:30-10:30pm Sat, 10:30am-2:30pm & 5-9pm Sun, cafe 8am-5pm Mon-Fri, 9am-5pm Sat, 9am-9pm Sun) takes all-natural ingredients and turns them into tasty small plates, such as bacon-wrapped dates stuffed with chorizo, and big ones like the zinfandel-braised short rib. **Lukshon** (📞310-202-6808; www.lukshon.com; 3239 Helms Ave; dishes $10-34; 🕙11:30am-2:30pm & 5:30-10pm Tue-Thu, to 10:30pm Fri & Sat) serves upscale Southeast Asian flavors in high design environs, and you can get craft beer and sourdough crusted pizza at the slab marble bar at **Wildcraft** (📞310-815-8100; www.wildcraftpizza.com; 9725 Culver Blvd; pizzas $14-20; 🕙noon-3pm & 5-9pm Mon, to 10pm Thu-Thu, to 10:30pm Fri, 11am-3pm & 5-10:30pm Sat, 11am-3pm & 5-9pm Sun).

❺ Kirk Douglas Theatre

An old-timey movie house has been recast as the 300-seat **Kirk Douglas Theatre** (📞213-628-2772; www.center theatregroup.org; 9820 Washington Blvd). Since opening in 2004, it has become an integral part of Culver City's growing arts scene, showcasing new plays by local playwrights.

❻ Turning Point Museum

Newly housed in the former National Guard Armory, under-the-radar **Wende Museum** (📞310-216-1600; www. wendemuseum.org; 10808 Culver Blvd; admission free; 🕙10am-9pm Fri, to 5pm Sat & Sun; 🅿) stands out for its vast, yet niche collection. German for 'turning point', Wende collects anything and everything made, bought, sold and created in Soviet Bloc countries from the end of WWII to the fall of the Berlin Wall.

Explore

Santa Monica

Santa Monica is LA's cute, alluring, hippie-chic little sister, its karmic counterbalance and, to many, its salvation. Surrounded by LA on three sides and the Pacific on the fourth, SaMo is a place where real-life Lebowskis sip white Russians next to martini-swilling Hollywood producers, celebrity chefs dine at family-owned taquerias, and soccer moms and career bachelors shop at abundant farmers markets.

The Sights in a Day

☀ Enjoy breakfast at the beloved **Huckleberry** (p96), where the bakery is always rocking and the coffee sublime. Then walk down Wilshire Bl to the bluffs at **Palisades Park** (p94) to survey the endless ocean. Stroll south to the **Santa Monica Pier** (p90) to hop on the Ferris wheel or roller coaster at **Pacific Park** (p91), or hang with the anglers. On the sand on **Santa Monica Beach** (p91), stick your toes in the cool Pacific or rent a bicycle.

☀ Hit **Tacos Por Favor** (p97) for authentic taqueria flavor and continue east to browse the exhibits at **California Heritage Museum** (p94) before taking in the scene among the shops and street performers of **Third Street Promenade** (p101). Head back to Palisades Park for a classic California sunset.

☾ A high-flying Southeast Asian dinner awaits at **Cassia** (p95), named one of America's best restaurants. Then head for a precision-poured cocktail at **Copa d'Oro** (p99) or a swanky night clubbing at the **Bungalow** (p98).

Top Sights

Santa Monica Pier & Beach (p90)

♥ Best of Santa Monica

Eating
Cassia (p95)

Drinking
Onyx (p99)

Chez Jay (p98)

Getting There

🚈 **Train** The **Metro Expo Line** light-rail connects Santa Monica with Downtown LA in about 50 minutes.

🚌 **Bus** Santa Monica's **Big Blue Bus** is the best choice for transport within Santa Monica, with service south to Venice and east to Westwood and Downtown LA.

🚲 **Bike** Breeze Bike Share stations are located all over town, in addition to numerous bike-rental facilities.

🚗 **Taxi/Ride Share** From LAX Airport, your best bet is a taxi or ride-hailing service such as **Uber** or **Lyft**. Service by Big Blue Bus requires connections.

Top Sights
Santa Monica Pier & Beach

Once the very end of the iconic Route 66, and still the object of a tourist love affair, the Santa Monica Pier dates back to 1908 and is the city's most compelling landmark. There are arcades, carnival games, a vintage carousel (p94), a Ferris wheel, a roller coaster and an **aquarium** (☎310-393-6149; www.healthebay.org; 1600 Ocean Front Walk; adult/child $5/free; ⏲2-6pm Tue-Fri, 12:30-6pm Sat & Sun; 👪; Ⓜ Expo Line to Downtown Santa Monica). The pier comes alive with free concerts (Twilight Concert Series; p100) and outdoor movies in the summertime.

◉ Map p92, A4

☎310-458-8901

www.santamonicapier.org

👪

Ferris wheel at Pacific Park

Pacific Park

Kids and kids within get their kicks on Santa Monica Pier at this small, classic Americana **amusement park** (☎310-260-8744; www.pacpark.com; 380 Santa Monica Pier; per ride $5-10, all-day pass adult/child under 8yr $32/18; ⏰daily, seasonal hours vary; ♿; ⓂExpo Line to Downtown Santa Monica), with a solar-powered Ferris wheel, tame roller coaster, family-friendly rides, midway games and food stands. Check the website for discount passes.

The Beach

There are endless ways to enjoy this 3.5-mile **stretch of sand** (☎310-458-8411; www.smgov.net/portals/beach; 🚌Big Blue Bus 1), running from Venice Beach in the south to Will Rogers State Beach in the north. Sunbathing and swimming are obvious options, but you can also reserve time on a beach volleyball court, work out at the **Original Muscle Beach** (www.musclebeach.net; 1800 Ocean Front Walk; ⏰sunrise-sunset) or, for more cerebral pursuits, settle in at a first-come first-served chess table at **International Chess Park** (☎310-458-8450; www.smgov.net; Ocean Front Walk at Seaside Tce; ⏰sunrise-sunset), just south of the Santa Monica pier.

South Bay Bicycle Trail

The **South Bay Bicycle Trail** (⏰sunrise-sunset; ♿) parallels the sand for most of the 22 miles between Will Rogers State Beach on the north end of Santa Monica and Torrance County Beach in the south.

☑ Top Tips

▶ Take in the view: the pier extends almost a quarter-mile over the Pacific, so you can stroll to the edge, hang out among the motley anglers and lose yourself contemplating the rolling, blue-green sea.

✗ Take a Break

Dogtown Coffee (www.dogtowncoffee.com; 2003 Main St; ⏰5:30am-5pm Mon-Fri, from 6:30am Sat & Sun) is in the old Zephyr surf-shop headquarters, where skateboarding was invented during a 1970s drought that emptied pools across LA. It brews great coffee and makes a mean breakfast burrito, the preferred nutritional supplement of surfers the world over. And it's open for dawn patrol. Fun fact: Dogtown is the nickname bestowed by skateboarders on the southern part of Santa Monica and into Venice.

Sights

Carousel   CAROUSEL

1 ◉ Map p92, A4

A National Historic Landmark at the
beginning of the pier, the 1916 Hippo-
drome building housing the carousel
appeared in the movie *The Sting*. The
44 horses (and one rabbit and one
goat), calliope and traditional soda
fountain continue to charm adults
and kids. (☑310-394-8042; Santa Monica
Pier; ⏱hours vary; ♿)

Annenberg Community
Beach House   BEACH

2 ◉ Map p92, A1

Like a fancy beach club for the rest of
us, the sleek and attractive city-owned
Annenberg Community Beach House
was built on actress Marion Davies'
estate. It opens to the public on a
first-come-first-served basis. It has a
lap pool, lounge chairs, yoga classes,
beach volleyball, fitness room and art
gallery.

There's a cafe nearby, set on a sweet
stretch of Santa Monica Beach. Opening hours are seasonal; see the website
for details. (☑310-458-4904; www.annen
bergbeachhouse.com; 415 Pacific Coast Hwy;
per hour/day Nov-Mar $3/8, Apr-Oct $3/12,
pool admission adult/senior/child $10/5/4)

Palisades Park   PARK

3 ◉ Map p92, B3

Perhaps it's appropriate that Route 66,
America's most romanticized byway,
ends at this gorgeous cliffside park
perched dramatically on the edge of
the continent. Stretching 1.5 miles
north from the pier, this palm-dotted
greenway sees a mix of resident home-
less people, joggers and tourists taking
in the ocean and pier views. Sunsets
are priceless. (☑800-544-5319; Ocean
Ave between Colorado Ave & San Vicente Blvd;
admission free; ⏱5am-midnight)

California
Heritage Museum   MUSEUM

4 ◉ Map p92, B7

For a trip back in time, check out the
latest exhibit at this museum housed
in one of Santa Monica's few surviving
grand Victorian mansions – this one
built in 1894. Curators do a wonderful
job presenting pottery, colorful tiles,
craftsman furniture, folk art, vintage
surfboards and other fine collectibles
in as dynamic a fashion as possible.
(☑310-392-8537; www.californiaheritage
museum.org; 2612 Main St; adult/student &
senior/under 12yr $5/3/free; ⏱11am-4pm
Wed-Sun; ℗; ☐Big Blue Bus line 8, Metro
line 733)

Edgemar   NOTABLE BUILDING

5 ◉ Map p92, B7

A shopping mall like no other, this
was designed by Frank Gehry, whose
signature LA work is Walt Disney
Concert Hall (p120). It's a relatively
early design of his from the 1980s, but
you'll see signature poured-in-place
concrete, metal fencing and a soaring
tower. Grab a coffee or ice cream at

Carousel on Santa Monica Pier

Peet's or Ben & Jerry's and sit down to enjoy it near the fountain in the courtyard. (📞310-924-9199; www.edgemar. com; 2415-2449 Main St)

Eating

Santa Monica Farmers Markets
MARKET $

6 🍽 Map p92, B3

You haven't really experienced Santa Monica until you've explored one of its weekly outdoor farmers markets stocked with organic fruits, vegetables, flowers, baked goods and freshly shucked oysters. The Mac Daddy is the Wednesday market, around the intersection of 3rd and Arizona – it's the biggest and arguably the best for fresh produce, and often patrolled by local chefs. (www.smgov.net/portals/farm ersmarket; Arizona Ave, btwn 2nd & 3rd Sts; 🕐Arizona Ave: 8:30am-1:30pm Wed, 8am-1pm Sat, Main St: 8:30am-1:30pm Sun; 👶)

Cassia
SOUTHEAST ASIAN $$$

7 🍽 Map p92, C3

Ever since it opened in 2015, open, airy Cassia has made about every local and national 'best' list of LA restaurants. Chef Bryant Ng draws on his Chinese-Singaporean heritage in dishes such as kaya toast (with coconut jam, butter and a slow-cooked egg), 'sunbathing' prawns, and the encompassing Vietnamese *pot-au-feu*: short-rib stew, veggies, bone marrow and delectable accompaniments. (☎310-393-6699; 1314 7th St; appetizers $12-24, mains $18-77; ☺5-10pm Sun-Thu, until 11pm Fri & Sat; P)

Huckleberry

CAFE $

8 | Map p92, D3

Part of the epicurean family from the couple behind Cassia (p95), Huckleberry's Zoe Nathan devises some of the most exquisite pastries in the city: salted caramel bars, crostatas bursting with blueberries, maple-bacon biscuits, and pumpkin and ginger tea cakes. A simple fried-egg sandwich goes gourmet with Niman Ranch bacon, Gruyère, arugula and aioli.

(☎310-451-2311; www.huckleberrycafe. com; 1014 Wilshire Blvd; mains $10-14; ☺8am-5pm)

Fig

BISTRO $$$

9 | Map p92, B3

Set poolside at the Fairmont Hotel, and conceived with a coastal organic ethos, Fig sources many ingredients from the twice-weekly farmers market down the street. We love the 'bread balloon' with choice of spreads (hummus, eggplant salad etc) and the veggie-forward menu that's inflected with Middle Eastern tastes (lamb sausage pizza, wood-grilled fish with tahini). (☎310-319-3111; www.figsantam onica.com; 101 Wilshire Blvd, Fairmont Miramar Hotel; mains lunch $13-24, dinner $18-34; ☺7am-2pm & 5-10pm Mon-Fri, 7am-2:30pm & 5-10pm Sat & Sun)

Santa Monica Seafood

SEAFOOD $$

10 | Map p92, C3

The best seafood market in Southern California offers a tasty oyster bar and market cafe, where you can sample delicious chowder, salmon burgers, albacore melts, oysters on the half shell and pan-roasted cod. (☎310-393-5244; www.santamonicaseafood.com; 1000 Wilshire Blvd; appetizers $7-15, mains $14-30; ☺9am-9pm Mon-Sat, to 8pm Sun; P)

Satdha

THAI, VEGAN $

11 | Map p92, C6

This vegan Thai restaurant draws fans from all over town to an unassuming

Santa Monica Farmers Markets (p95)

stretch of Lincoln Blvd for vibrant dishes such as endive cups filled with cashew 'tuna', coconut, ginger, lemongrass, peanuts and more; green papaya or snappea salads; beet-dyed noodles; and eggplant served catfish-style in curry paste. The vibe is comfy, contemporary and friendly. (☑310-450-6999; www.satdhakitchen.com; 2218 Lincoln Blvd; mains $11-13; ⏱11am-3pm & 5-9:30pm Tue-Sun; ☑)

Ye Olde King's Head   BRITISH $$

12 Map p92, B4

Fancy LA's best fish and chips? Or some bangers and mash, shepherd's pie or curry? This been-there-forever pub is a slice of 'jolly old' on the left coast. Breakfasts span beans on toast to the 'king size English breakfast' (eggs, bacon, sausage etc – basically the full monty). (☑310-451-1402; www.yeoldekingshead.com; 116 Santa Monica Blvd; breakfast dishes $6-14, sandwiches & salads $10-15, mains $14-23; ⏱9am-10pm Mon-Wed, to 11pm Thu & Fri, 8am-11pm Sat, 8am-10pm Sun)

Sunny Blue   JAPANESE $

13 Map p92, B7

In Japan, *omusubi* (rice balls, aka *onigiri*) are an everyday staple, and this counter-service shop aims to make them popular Stateside. Before your eyes, the cheerful staff stuffs fluffy rice with dozens of fillings such as miso beef, spicy salmon and chicken curry – and veggie-friendly options like miso mushroom and hijiki seaweed – then

wraps it in a crunchy *nori* seaweed wrapper. (☑310-399-9030; www.sunnyblueinc.com; 2728 Main St; rice balls from $3.15; ⏱11am-8pm Mon-Thu, to 9pm Fri & Sat, to 7pm Sun;)

Tacos Por Favor   MEXICAN $

14 Map p92, D5

This beloved counter-service hole-in-the-wall is dingy, hot and often crowded, with concrete floors, food served on paper plates and a menu so vast that you and your besties could eat breakfast, lunch and dinner here for a week and never order the same thing twice. At least order *carne asada*, shrimp and chicken tacos and burritos. (☑310-392-5768; www.tacosporfavor.net; 1408 Olympic Blvd; tacos & burritos $2.75-9.50, combination plates $7.50-14;

Rat Pack to Brat Pack

Rocking since 1959, **Chez Jay** (www.chezjays.com; 1657 Ocean Ave; ⏱11:45am-2pm & 5:30-9:30pm Mon-Fri, 9am-1:45pm & 5:30-9:30pm Sat & Sun) is a nautical-themed dive that's seen its share of Hollywood intrigue from the Rat Pack to the Brat Pack. To this day it's dark and dank and all the more glorious for it. The classic steak and seafood menu's not bad, either.

⏱8am-8pm; Ⓜ Expo Line to 17th St/Santa Monica College)

Stella Barra   PIZZA $$

15   Map p92, B6

One of our favorite places on Main, it does a white pizza loaded with crispy kale, and another with prosciutto and egg on a bed of mozzarella and Gruyère. It makes its own pork sausage and the salads are tasty. Even the breakfast pizzas work. So do the $5 bloodies. (☎310-396-9250; www.stellabarra.com; 2000 Main St; salads $10-11, pizzas $13-16; ⏱5pm-midnight Mon-Thu, 11am-1am Fri, 10am-1am Sat, 10am-10pm Sun)

Library Alehouse   PUB FOOD $$

16 Map p92, B8

Locals gather for the food as much as the beer at this wood-paneled gastro-pub with a cozy outdoor patio in the back. Angus burgers, fish tacos and

hearty salads sate the 30-something, postwork regulars, while 29 hand-crafted microbrews keep 'em hanging around till midnight. (☎310-314-4855; www.libraryalehouse.com; 2911 Main St; mains $8-19; ⏱11:30am-midnight Mon-Fri, from 11am Sat & Sun)

Drinking

The Bungalow   LOUNGE

17   Map p92, B3

A Brent Bolthouse nightspot, the in-door-outdoor lounge at the Fairmont Miramar was one of the hottest nights out in LA when it burst onto the scene a couple of years ago. It's since settled down, and like most Westside spots can be too dude-centric late in the evening, but the setting is elegant and there's still beautiful mischief to be found here. (www.thebungalowsm.com; 101 Wilshire Blvd, Fairmont Miramar Hotel; ⏱5pm-2am Mon-Fri, noon-2am Sat, noon-10pm Sun)

Basement Tavern   BAR

18 Map p92, B7

A creative speakeasy, housed in the basement of the Victorian, and our favorite well in Santa Monica. We love it for its craftsman cocktails, cozy booths, island bar and nightly live-music calendar that features blues, jazz, bluegrass and rock bands. It gets way too busy on weekends for our taste, but weeknights can be special.

Twilight Concert Series (p100)

www.basementtavern.com; 2640 Main St; ⏰5pm-2am)

Onyx   ROOFTOP BAR

19 📍 Map p92, B3

Santa Monica's only indoor-outdoor roof bar has a swinging-'70s, Studio 54 vibe – brass-plated fireplace, hexgonal ceiling tiles – a bar made of a giant onyx slab (get it?) and cocktails such as the TamieTini (Ketel One, basil, passion fruit and cava) and the Shangri-La Mojito. But we most love surveying the view from the Pier to Malibu from seven stories up. (www.shangrila-hotel.com; 1301 Ocean Ave, Hotel Shangri-La; ⏰4pm-midnight Mon-Wed, to

2am Thu, 3pm-2am Fri & Sat, 3pm-midnight Sun)

Copa d'Oro   BAR

20 📍 Map p92, B4

The cocktail menu was created by the talented Vincenzo Marianella – a man who knows his spirits and has trained his team to concoct addictive cocktails from a well of top-end spirits and a produce bin of fresh herbs, fruits, juices and a few veggies. The rock tunes and the smooth, dark ambience don't hurt. (www.copadoro.com; 217 Broadway; ⏰5:30pm-midnight Mon-Wed, to 2am Thu-Sat)

Entertainment

Twilight Concert Series
LIVE MUSIC

21 Map p92, A5

This beloved local institution brings Santa Monicans of all stripes to rock out by the thousands on the pier and on the sand below, gigging local to world-famous names. Recently: Mavis Staples, Save Ferris and the Psychedelic Furs. (www.santamonicapier.org/twilight; admission free; ⏰7-10pm Thu Jul-early Sep)

Harvelle's
BLUES

22 ⭐ Map p92, B4

This dark blues grotto has been packing 'em in since 1931, but somehow still manages to feel like a well-kept secret. There are no big-name acts here, but the quality is usually high. Sunday's Toledo Show mixes soul, jazz and cabaret, and Wednesday night brings the always-funky House of Vibe All-Stars. (☎310-395-1676; www.harvelles.com; 1432 4th St; cover $5-15)

Broad Stage
THEATER

23 ⭐ Map p92, D3

A 499-seat, state-of-the-art theater anchors Santa Monica College's striking, modernist performing-arts complex, which is a satellite campus on its own. Touring shows bring everything from new interpretations of classic Shakespeare to one-man productions, edgy plays and classical and world-music performances. (☎310-434-3200; www.thebroadstage.com; 1310 11th St)

Aero Theater
CINEMA

24 ⭐ Map p92, D1

Santa Monica's original movie theater (c 1940) is now operated by American Cinematheque (p30), where it screens old and neo classics and offers Q&A sessions with bigwigs from time to time. Check its online calendar for upcoming shows. (www.americancinematheque.com; 1328 Montana Ave)

Shopping

Puzzle Zoo
GAMES

25 🔒 Map p92, B4

Those searching galaxy-wide for the caped Lando Calrissian action figure, look no more. Puzzle Zoo stocks every imaginable *Star Wars* or anime figurine this side of Endor. There's also an encyclopedic selection of puzzles,

Top Tip
Magicopolis

Aspiring Harry Potters won't be the only ones who enjoy the comedy-laced sleight-of-hand, levitation and other illusions performed by Steve Spills and cohorts in this intimate space of **Magicopolis** (☎310-451-2241; www.magicopolis.com; 1418 4th St; tickets $24-34; ⏰8pm Fri & Sat, 2pm Sat & Sun; 👶). Escapes from reality last about 1½ hours and there's even a small shop for all your wizard supplies.

oard games and toys. Kids adore it.
📞310-393-9201; www.puzzlezoo.com; 1411
hird St Promenade; ⏰10am-10pm Sun-Thu,
⏰ 11pm Fri & Sat; 🚻)

ital Hemp
FASHION & ACCESSORIES

26 🔒 Map p92, B6

A boutique stocked with designer,
cofriendly hemp goods made in
Downtown LA. It has fitted tees,
hinos, hoodies and more, perfectly
uited to the coastal casual look.
📞310-450-2260; www.vitalhemp.com; 2305
Main St; ⏰10am-6pm)

en Women
ART

27 🔒 Map p92, B7

t sells the art, folk art and crafts
rom a cooperative of 21 (it used to be
0) female artists. Always changing,
ut look for works in ceramic, wood,
extiles, jewelry and more. (📞310-314-
152; www.tenwomengallery.com; 2651 Main
t; ⏰noon-5pm Sun & Mon, 11am-6pm Tue &
hu, 11am-4pm Wed, 10am-6pm Fri & Sat)

reat Labels
FASHION & ACCESSORIES

28 🔒 Map p92, D3

ensational secondhand couture
nd designer hand-me-downs from
elebrity consigners. There's Oscar
nd Golden Globe gowns, elegant
andbags, shoes and accessories from
ucci, Prada, Jimmy Choo and Dior.
f you've ever wanted to pay $250 for
four-figure dress, come here. (📞310-

 Local Life

Shopping in Downtown Santa Monica

Stretching for three long blocks
between Broadway and Wilshire
Blvd, **Third Street Promenade** (3rd
St between Broadway & Wilshire Blvd)
offers carefree, car-free strolling
accompanied by topiaries, fountains and street performers. **Santa
Monica Place** (www.santamonicaplace.
com; 395 Santa Monica Pl; ⏰10am-
9pm Mon-Sat, 11am-8pm Sun), at the
south end of the Promenade, offers
posher national and international
chains: All Saints, Michael Kors, Tif-
fany and flagship Uniqlo and Nike
stores, alongside Bloomingdales
and Nordstrom.

451-2277; www.greatlabels.com; 1126 Wilshire
Blvd; ⏰10am-6pm Mon-Sat, 11am-5pm Sun)

Aura Shop
NEW AGE

29 🔒 Map p92, B8

Well, you *are* in California so you
might as well get your aura read. Yes,
auras do exist (it's that heat energy
radiating off your skin) and the color
trails they leave behind signify…
something, or so we're told. Just get
the aura photo and the reading and
believe it or not. Also sells books, candles and crystals. (📞310-584-9998; www.
aurashop.com; 2914 Main St; ⏰11am-6pm
Mon-Sat, to 5pm Sun)

Top Sights
Malibu

Getting There

🚗 The I-10 Fwy becomes California Hwy 1 north in Santa Monica. Follow it to paradise.

🚌 MTA's Malibu Express line 534 leaves from Fairfax Ave and Washington Blvd.

Everyone needs a little Malibu. Here's a moneyed, stylish yet laid-back beach town and celebrity enclave that rambles for 27 miles along the Pacific Coast Hwy, blessed with the stunning natural beauty of its coastal mountains, pristine coves, wide sweeps of golden sand and epic waves.

Surfrider Beach and Malibu Pier

El Matador State Beach

El Matador (📞818-880-0363; 32215 Pacific Coast Hwy; **P**) is arguably Malibu's most stunning beach. Park on the bluffs and stroll down a trail to sandstone rock towers that rise from emerald coves. Topless sunbathers stroll through the tides and dolphins breech the surface beyond the waves.

Getty Villa

Stunningly perched on an ocean-view hillside, the replica 1st-century Roman **Getty Villa** (📞310-430-7300; www.getty.edu; 17985 Pacific Coast Hwy, Pacific Palisades; admission free; ⏱10am-5pm Wed-Mon; **P**♿; 🚌line 534 to Coastline Dr) is an exquisite, 64-acre showcase for Greek, Roman and Etruscan antiquities. Galleries, courtyards and lushly landscaped gardens ensconce all manner of art, plus brain-bending geometric configurations in the Hall of Colored Marbles.

Malibu Pier

The pier (www.malibupier.com; 23000 Pacific Coast Hwy; ⏱6:30am-sunset) marks the beginning of Malibu's commercial heart. It's open for strolling and license-free fishing (note the brackets for your rod and reel) and delivers fine views of surfers riding waves off Surfrider Beach. You can rent a rod and reel ($14 for two hours) and buy bait ($5) here, too.

Nobu Malibu

The **Malibu outpost** (📞310-317-9140; www.noburestaurants.com; 22706 Pacific Coast Hwy; dishes $8-46; ⏱noon-10pm Mon-Thu, 9am-11pm Fri & Sat, to 10pm Sun; **P**) of Chef Nobu Matsuhisa's empire of luxe Japanese restaurants is consistently one of LA's hot spots, with a high celeb quotient. It's a cavernous, modern wood chalet with a long sushi bar and a dining room that spills onto a patio overlooking the swirling sea.

☑ Top Tips

▶ Unless you strike gold and find free parking on Pacific Coast Hwy, midday parking in lots varies by the day and the season, between $6 and $15.

▶ It's best to explore Malibu midweek, especially in summer. That way you'll have the roads and the beaches mostly to yourself.

▶ Malibu is an ideal family destination. Kids can get busy getting dirty on the beach or in the hills and mom can shop and in the swanky shops off Cross Creek Rd.

✗ Take a Break

In an unbeatable location on Malibu Pier, the whitewashed dining rooms at **Malibu Farm** (📞310-456-1112; www.malibu-farm.com; 23000 Pacific Coast Hwy; mains breakfast $11-16, lunch & dinner $13-32; ⏱7am-9pm, until 10pm Sat; 🚌MTA line 534) are beachy keen for munching on farm-to-table brunches, pizzas, and sandwiches. They also have a more casual cafe.

Explore

Venice

If you were born too late, and have always been a little jealous of the hippie heyday, come down to the Boardwalk and inhale a (not just) incense-scented whiff of Venice, a boho beach town and longtime haven for artists, new agers, road-weary tramps, freaks and free spirits. This is where Jim Morrison and the Doors lit their fire and where Arnold Schwarzenegger pumped himself to stardom. These days the Old Venice spirit endures.

The Sights in a Day

☼ Work off your hangover at **Eggslut** (p110) and then head out to the beach for a morning swim or surf. Welcome to Venice, man.

☼ Head over to **Abbot Kinney Blvd** (p109) for a gourmet vegan lunch at **Plant Food + Wine** (p111) served in the back herb garden, before browsing the shops down the block. As the afternoon heats up, so does the action on the **boardwalk** (p106), an only-in-LA pageant of street performers, vendors, graffiti artists, skateboarders and more.

☾ Grab a table at **High** (p112) rooftop lounge to watch the sun set over the ocean, before dinner at **Gjelina** (p112) and a nightcap at **Townhouse & Delmonte Speakeasy** (p113).

⊙ Top Sight
Venice Boardwalk (p106)

💗 Best of Los Angeles
Eating
Gjelina (p112)

Eggslut (p110)

Salt & Straw (p110)

Shopping
Abbot Kinney Blvd (p109)

Aviator Nation (p115)

General Admission (p114)

Getting There

🚌 **Bus** Santa Monica's Big Blue Bus lines 3 and 18 travel along Lincoln Blvd and Abbot Kinney Blvd respectively. Line 3 connects to the LAX Transit Center.

Top Sights
Venice Boardwalk

Life in Venice moves to a different rhythm and nowhere more so than on the famous Venice Boardwalk, officially known as Ocean Front Walk. It's a freak show, a human zoo and a wacky carnival alive with Hula-Hoop magicians, old-timey jazz combos, solo distorted garage rockers and artists (good and bad) – as far as LA experiences go, it's a must.

Ocean Front Walk

👁 Map p108, A3

Venice Pier to Rose Ave

Venice Skatepark

Murals

Venice Beach has long been associated with street art, and for decades there was a struggle between outlaw artists and law enforcement. Art won out and the tagged-up towers and the free-standing concrete wall of the **Venice Beach Art Walls** (www.veniceartwalls.com; 1800 Ocean Front Walk, Venice; ⏰10am-5pm Sat & Sun; 👶), right on the beach, have been covered by graffiti artists from 1961 to the present.

Muscle Beach

Gym rats with an exhibitionist streak can get a tan and a workout at this famous outdoor **gym** (📞310-399-2775; musclebeach.net; 1800 Ocean Front Walk, Venice; per day $10; ⏰8am-7pm Mon-Sat, 10am-4pm Sun Apr-Sep, shorter hours rest of year) right on the Venice Boardwalk, where Arnold Schwarzenegger and Franco Columbu once bulked up.

Venice Skatepark

Long the destination of local skate punks, the concrete at this **skate park** (www.veniceskatepark. com; 1500 Ocean Front Walk, Venice; ⏰dawn-dusk) has now been molded and steel-fringed into 17,000 sq ft of vert, tranny and street terrain with unbroken ocean views. The old-school-style skate run and the world-class pool are most popular for high flyers and gawking spectators. Great photo opps, especially as the sun sets.

☑ Top Tips

▶ The Sunday-afternoon drum circle draws hundreds of revelers for tribal jamming and spontaneous dancing on the grassy mounds (sometimes beats migrate to the sand, as well).

▶ During the summer, the Boardwalk is always alive. Off-season, there is still life around sunset when crowds gather at cafes, bars and on the bike path.

✗ Take a Break

No place melds Old Venice and New Venice like **Rose Cafe** (📞310-399-0711; www.rosecafevenice. com; 220 Rose Ave, Venice; breakfast $10-17, lunch mains $10-28, dinner mains $20-32; ⏰7am-10pm Tue-Thu, to 11pm Fri, 8am-11pm Sat, 8am-10pm Sun; 🅿👶). Established 1979, it was recently given a major, very welcome makeover. Display cases show off lovely salads, prepared dishes and pastries, which you can take to a hedge-framed patio, and there's a fancier sit-down garden section.

A

B

C

D

Santa
Monica
State Beach

3rd St

4th St

400 m
0.2 miles

1

11

Rose Ave

16

6 Binoculars
Building

Pacific Ave

5th Ave

6th Ave

7th Ave

Lincoln Blvd

3 Gold's Gym

Sunset Ave

10

Vernon Ave

Ocean Front Walk

Speedway

Main St

2nd St

Indiana Ave

2

20

Abbot
Kinney
Boulevard

Brooks Ave

Venice
Beach

1

Broadway St

Abbot Kinney Blvd

Westminster Ave

*Venice
Boardwalk*

Westminster Ave

9

San Juan Ave

24

California Ave

San Juan Ave

21

Santa Clara Ave

Electric Ave

3

Market St

22

17

7

19

15

14

Windward Ave

8

VENICE

13

Venice Way

Grand Blvd

23

12

LA Louver 5

Mildred Ave

Dell Ave

18

Electric Ave

4

C.A.V.E.

4

Speedway

N Venice Blvd

S Venice Blvd

P

2 Canal Park
*Venice
Canals*

Venice Canals

Santa
Monica
Bay

Dell Ave

Venice Way

5

South
Venice
Beach

For reviews see	
Top Sights	p106
Sights	p109
Eating	p110
Drinking	p112
Shopping	p114

Washington Blvd

Sights

Abbot Kinney Boulevard AREA

 1 Map p108, B2

Abbot Kinney, who founded Venice in the early 1900s, would probably be delighted to find that one of Venice's best-loved streets bears his name. Sort of a seaside Melrose with a Venetian flavor, the mile-long stretch of Abbot Kinney Blvd between Venice Blvd and Main St is full of upscale boutiques, galleries, lofts and sensational restaurants. A few years back, GQ named it America's coolest street, and that cachet has only grown since. (🚌 Big Blue Bus line 18)

Venice Canals AREA

2 Map p108, B4

Even many Angelenos have no idea that just a couple of blocks from the Boardwalk madness is an idyllic neighborhood that preserves 3 miles of Abbot Kinney's canals. The **Venice Canal Walk** threads past eclectic homes, over bridges and along waterways where ducks preen and locals lollygag in little rowboats. It's best accessed from either Venice or Washington Blvds.

Gold's Gym GYM

 3 Map p108, B1

There are gyms, then there's Gold's Gym, and *then* there's the original 1965 Gold's, the self-titled 'Mecca of Bodybuilding.' Generations have been lifting at the place that arguably started the fitness craze – no less than

Venice Canals

Arnold Schwarzenegger trained here for the iconic 1977 muscle-mania film *Pumping Iron*. Nowadays it also holds classes from kickboxing to pilates and zumba. (☎ 310-392-6004; www.goldsgym. com; 360 Hampton Dr (aka 2nd St); day/week/month pass $25/100/175; ⏰ 4am-midnight Mon-Fri, to 11pm Sat & Sun; 🚌 Big Blue Bus lines 1, 18)

LA Louver GALLERY

 4 Map p108, A4

The best art gallery in Venice, and arguably the best in LA, LA Louver was established by Peter Goulds in 1975, and since 1994 has been housed in a landmark building designed by Frederick Fisher. It's a modern and contemporary art gallery featuring

rotating, museum-quality exhibitions that show for five to six weeks. (☎310-822-4955; www.lalouver.com; 45 N Venice Blvd; admission free; ☺10am-6pm Tue-Sat)

C.A.V.E. GALLERY

5 Map p108, A4

One of our favorite Venice galleries, it specializes in single-artist exhibitions. When we passed, it hosted the works of Ralph Ziman, a South African–born artist who hung traditionally beaded machine guns to publicize the effects of conflict across Africa. He called it 'Ghosts.' The name is short for 'Center for Audio and Visual Expression.' (☎310-428-6837; www.cavegallery.net; 55 N Venice Blvd; ☺noon-6pm Wed-Sat, to 4pm Sun)

Binoculars Building NOTABLE BUILDING

6 Map p108, B1

Formerly known as the Chiat/Day Building, this Frank Gehry–designed office building is home to Google and,

Top Tip

Arts and Culture

Venice's collection of murals is second to none, modeled after **Jim Morrison** (Morning Shot; 1881 Speedway), **Van Gogh** (Ocean Front Walk, at Wavecrest Ave) and Botticelli's **Birth of Venus** (25 Windward Ave). On the high end, LA Louver (p109) is one of LA's most renowned galleries.

thanks to its eye-catching architecture and the Claes Oldenburg and Coosje van Bruggen sculpture out front (clue to its design in the name), makes for a fun photo stop on the north end of Venice. (340 Main St)

Eating

Eggslut BREAKFAST $

7 Map p108, A3

Westside outpost of the DTLA hipster foodie favorite. This cozy, post-industrial storefront's best seller is the Fairfax sandwich (a lovably gooey mess of scrambled eggs, caramelized onion and sriracha mayo) served in adorable mini paper bags. The name-sake 'eggslut' is a coddled egg nestled on top of potato purée in a glass jar and served with toasted crostini. (☎424-438-7818; www.eggslut.com; 1611 Pacific Ave; mains $7-9; ☺8am-4pm)

Salt & Straw ICE CREAM $

8 Map p108, C3

There always seems to be a line out the door at this branch of the hipster-cool Portland-based ice-cream fantasy land. Maybe it's because there's always something new to try: adventurous, seasonal flavors that change monthly – think farmers-market veggies to late-summer harvest. Check the website for current offerings. (☎310-310-8429; www.saltandstraw.com; 1537 Abbot Kinney Blvd; ice cream from $4; ☺10am-11pm)

Butcher's Daughter
VEGETARIAN, CAFE $$

9 Map p108, C3

Find yourself a seat around the central counter or facing busy Abbot Kinney to tuck in to stone-oven pizzas, handmade pastas and veggie faves such as whole roasted cauliflower and butternut squash risotto. It's Aussie-owned, meaning great coffee. Light, airy and fun. Welcome to California! (📞310-981-3004; www.thebutchersdaughter.com; 1205 Abbot Kinney Blvd; dishes $10-22; ⏰8am-10pm)

Gjusta
CALIFORNIAN $$

10 Map p108, B2

The folks behind the standard-setting Gjelina (p112) have opened this very casual, very gourmet, *very* Venice bakery, cafe and deli behind a nondescript storefront on a hidden side street. The menu changes regularly, but if we say lunches of chicken, cabbage and dumpling soup, house-cured charcuterie and fish (such as gravlax, smoked Wagyu brisket and leg of lamb), does that help? (📞310-314-0320; www.gjusta.com; 320 Sunset Ave; mains $7.50-20; ⏰7am-9pm; 🚌Big Blue Bus lines 1, 18)

Cerveteca
MEXICAN $$

11 Map p108, C1

A gourmet Mexican kitchen with fusion digressions (such as the chorizo burger and the mac-n-cheese with bacon). The patio is inviting, but so is the stylish interior, with a wide

marble bar, craftsman drafts (this is a *cerveteca,* or beer bar, after all) and global tunes on the sound system. (📞310-310-8937; www.cervetecala.com; 523 Rose Ave; mains $12-21; ⏰11:30am-11pm Mon-Fri, 10:30am-3pm & 4-11pm Sat & Sun)

Tasting Kitchen
ITALIAN $$$

12 Map p108, C4

From the salt-roasted branzino, to the porcini-crusted hangar steak, to the burger and the quail, it's all very good here. The pastas are especially good (that bucatini is a gift from the gods), as are the cocktails. Which is why it's almost always packed. Book ahead. (📞310-392-6644; www.thetastingkitchen.com; 1633 Abbot Kinney Blvd; mains $16-40; ⏰10:30am-2:30pm Sat & Sun, 5:30pm-midnight daily)

Gjelina
AMERICAN $$$

13 Map p108, C3

If one restaurant defines the new Venice, it's this. Carve out a slip on the communal table between the hipsters and yuppies, or get your own slab of wood on the elegant stone terrace and dine on imaginative small plates (raw yellowtail spiced with chili and mint and drenched in olive oil and blood orange) and sensational thin-crust, wood-fired pizza. (📞310-450-1429; www.gjelina.com; 1429 Abbot Kinney Blvd; veggies, salads & pizzas $10-18, large plates $15-45; ⏰8am-midnight; 🚼; 🚌Big Blue Bus line 18)

Drinking

High
ROOFTOP BAR

14 Map p108, A3

Venice's only rooftop bar is quite an experience, with 360-degree views

🔍 Local Life
Bike Like a Venetian
You've learned to eat, talk and appreciate art like a Venetian; now get around like one. **Linus** (📞310-301-1866; www.linusbike.com; 1817 Lincoln Blvd; ⏰11am-7pm; 🚌Big Blue Bus line 3), the ultimate Venice bike shop, assembles sturdy, steel-frame bikes. You can't carry a bike home with you, you say? It also sells enviable accessories such as bike bags, baskets, cup holders and even beer holsters.

from the shore to the Santa Monica Mountains – if you can take your eyes off the beautiful people. High serves creative seasonal cocktails (blood-orange julep, lemon apple hot toddy, Mexican hot chocolate with tequila) and dishes like beef or lamb sliders, mezze plates and crab dip. Reservations recommended. (📞424-214-1062; www.highvenice.com; Hotel Erwin, 1697 Pacific Ave; ⏰3-10pm Mon-Thu, to midnight Fri, noon-midnight Sat, noon-10pm Sun)

Intelligentsia Coffeebar
CAFE

15 Map p108, C3

In this hip, industrial, minimalist monument to the coffee gods, perfectionist baristas – who roam the central bar and command more steaming machines than seems reasonable – never short you on foam or caffeine, and the Cake Monkey scones and muffins are addictive. The tunnel-like front vestibule is an oh-so-SoCal chill space. (📞310-399-1233; www.intelligentsiacoffee.com; 1331 Abbot Kinney Blvd; ⏰6am-8pm Mon-Thu, to 10pm Fri, 7am-10pm Sat, 7am-8pm Sun; 📶; 🚌Big Blue Bus line 18)

Venice Ale House
PUB

16 Map p108, A1

A fun pub right on the Boardwalk on Venice's north end, blessed with ample patio seating for sunset people-watching, long boards suspended from the rafters, rock on the sound system, and plenty of local brews on tap. Beer flights are served in a

Townhouse & Delmonte Speakeasy

drilled-out skate deck, and the pub grub works. (www.venicealehouse.com; 2 Rose Ave; ⊙10am-midnight Mon-Thu, to 2am Fri, 9am-2am Sat, 9am-midnight Sun)

Townhouse & Delmonte Speakeasy BAR

17 🍷 Map p108, A3

Upstairs is a cool, dark and perfectly dingy bar with pool tables, booths and good booze. Downstairs is the speakeasy, where DJs spin pop, funk and electronic music, comics take the mic and jazz players set up and jam. It's a reliably good time almost any night. (www.townhousevenice.com; 52 Windward Ave; ⊙5pm-2am Mon-Fri, from noon Sat & Sun)

Venice Beach Wines WINE BAR

A sweet and cozy hideaway (see 11 ✕ Map p108, C1) with louvered benches and tables so close together you will commune with strangers. Here, you may sip international wines by the glass or bottle (including a complex and invigorating French syrah) and munch charcuterie, *pizzettas* and the like. (☎310-606-2529; www.venicebeachwines. com; 529 Rose Ave; ⊙4-11pm Mon-Thu, to midnight Fri, noon-midnight Sat, noon-11pm Sun)

Brig BAR

18 🍷 Map p108, C4

Old-timers remember this place as a divey pool hall owned by ex-boxer Babe Brandelli (that's him and his wife

---

---

on the outside mural). Now it's a bit sleeker and attracts a trendy mix of grown-up beach bums, arty professionals and professional artists. On **First Fridays** (www.abbotkinneyfirstfridays.com; 5-11pm 1st Fri each month), the parking lot attracts a fleet of LA's famed food trucks. (www.thebrig.com; 1515 Abbot Kinney Blvd; 4pm-2am Mon-Wed, from 2pm Thu & Fri, from noon Sat & Sun)

Toms Flagship Store
CAFE

19 Map p108, C3

You know Toms, which made its name selling fun, slip-on canvas shoes and giving a pair away to underprivileged kids overseas for each pair sold in the States? Well, its flagship store doubles as a very chill cafe. Out back are a lawn, fireplace, shared tables and lounge seating in the sun and shade. A great hang. (310-314-9700; www.toms.com; 1344 Abbot Kinney Blvd; 7am-9pm Mon-Sat, to 8pm Sun; 🛜📶; Big Blue Bus line 18)

Shopping

General Admission
CLOTHING, ACCESSORIES

20 🔒 Map p108, B2

A block from the Abbot Kinney strip, this shop sells coastal-cool clothing and accessories, from sage-green Converse sneakers to surfboards, sunglasses and a line of watches and ineffably chic towels with art prints. As if it needed more hipster cred, it also operates a coffee bar across the street in an old Airstream trailer. (310-399-1051; www.generaladmission.us; 52 Brooks Ave; 11am-7pm)

Mystic Journey
SPIRITUALITY

This spot (see 23 🔒 Map p108, C4) serves all manner of spirituality, from Hindu to Wiccan, magic to no religion at all, with books, ritual objects, sound bells and bowls, crystals, self-improvement slogans and teas that support your chakras. A back room hosts lectures and events. As Abbot Kinney gentrifies, it's great to know that this very Old Venice institution continues to flourish. (📞310-399-7070; www.mysticjourneybookstore.com; 1624 Abbot Kinney Blvd; ⏰10am-8pm Sun-Thu, until 11pm Fri & Sat)

Waraku   SHOES

21 🔒 Map p108, C3

Waraku is a compact, Japanese-owned shop for shoe lovers. It blends Far East couture with mainstream street brands such as Puma and Converse. Some 60% of the shoes are imported from Japan, the rest are domestic limited editions. (📞310-452-5300; www.warakuusa.com; 1225 Abbot Kinney Blvd; ⏰10am-7pm; 🚌Big Blue Bus line 18)

Aviator Nation   CLOTHING

22 🔒 Map p108, C3

Coastal-chic hoodies, tees and blankets, even guitar picks come emblazoned with the signature stripes of yellow, orange and red. Behind the store is an awesome chill space with a DJ station, ping-pong table and plenty of couches to chill and listen to the bands it sometimes brings in. (📞310-396-9100; www.aviatornation.com; 1224 Abbot Kinney Blvd; ⏰10am-8pm)

Alexis Bittar   JEWELRY

23 🔒 Map p108, C4

High-end women's jewelry known for Bittar's use of lucite, which is hand-carved and painted in his Brooklyn studio. Some of it looks like stone. He started by selling it on the streets in Manhattan, where he was picked up by the MOMA store. (📞310-452-6901; www.alexisbittar.com; 1612 Abbot Kinney Blvd; ⏰11am-7pm Mon-Sat, noon-6pm Sun)

Burro   GIFTS & SOUVENIRS

One of our favorite shops (see **8** ❌ Map p108, C3) on Abbot Kinney deals in quality aromatherapy candles, art books, a smattering of boho-chic attire for ladies, fair-trade beach bags from India and beaded jewelry. It serves tots at the kid's store two doors down. (www.burrogoods.com; 1409 Abbot Kinney Blvd; ⏰10am-7pm; 🚌Big Blue Bus line 18)

Strange Invisible   PERFUME

24 🔒 Map p108, C3

Organic, intoxicating perfumes crafted from wild and natural ingredients, with names such as Aquarian Rose and Fair Verona, although some are gender neutral. Also sells dark chocolate. (📞310-314-1505; www.siperfumes.com; 1138 Abbot Kinney Blvd; ⏰11am-7pm Mon-Sat, noon-6pm Sun; 🚌Big Blue Bus line 18)

Local Life
Manhattan Beach, Beyond the Sand

A bastion of surf music and the birthplace of beach volleyball, Manhattan Beach may have gone chic, but that salty-dog heart still beats. Yes, the downtown area along Manhattan Beach Blvd has seen an explosion of trendy restaurants and boutiques, but the real action is beach-side, where the bikinis are small, the waves kind and the smiles as oversized as those sunglasses.

Getting There

🚗 Two exits off I-405 serve Manhattan Beach, including Rosecrans Blvd and Inglewood Ave, which merges with Manhattan Beach Blvd.

🚌 MTA 126

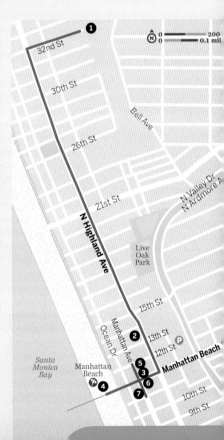

❶ Sweat & Tumble at Sand Dune Park

Sand Dune Park (📞 310-802-5448; www.citymb.info; cnr 33rd St & Bell Ave; admission $1; ⏰ by reservation from 8am daily, closing hours vary; 👪) requires reservations if you wish to access the long, deep 100ft-high natural sand dune. Adults enjoy their requisite running/suffering here. The kids will love hurling themselves down the dune again and again.

❷ Uncle Bill's Pancake House

Sexy surfers, tottering toddlers and gabbing girlfriends – everybody comes to **Uncle Bill's** (📞 310-545-5177; www.unclebills.net; 1305 N Highland Ave; dishes $8-15; ⏰ 6am-3pm Mon-Fri, from 7am Sat & Sun; 👪) for the famous pancakes and big fat omelettes.

❸ Photo Bomb

No surf, sport or music nut should miss the dazzling work on display at **Bo Bridges Gallery** (📞 310-937-3764; www.bobridgesgallery.com; 1108 Manhattan Ave; ⏰ 11am-7pm, extended hours in summer). Bridges made his name in the water shooting the likes of Kelly Slater at Pipeline, and parlayed that into mainstream sport and pop-culture success. You'll see plenty of famous faces on the wall.

❹ Hit the Beach

Ditch the shoes on this wide sweep of **golden sand** (www.citymb.info), where you'll find pick-up volleyball courts, a pier with breathtaking blue sea views from the edge, consistent sandy bottom surf and a giddy, pretty population that still can't believe they get to live here.

❺ MB Post

Trendy but friendly and unvarnished, **MB Post** (📞 310-545-5405; www.eatmbpost.com; 1142 Manhattan Ave; small plates $9-13, mains $11-39; ⏰ 5-10pm Mon-Thu, 11:30am-10:30pm Fri, 10am-10:30pm Sat, 10am-10pm Sun; 👪) offers globally inspired tapas. Walk in and dine at the long communal tables in the bar, or make a reservation and get close at a small table in the dining room.

❻ Indulge Your Ice Cream Addiction

There's a damn good reason the hordes are lined up along the wall and out the door of **Manhattan Beach Creamery** (📞 310-372-1155; www.mbcreamery.com; 1120 Manhattan Ave; ice creams $4-7; ⏰ 10am-10pm Sun-Thu, to 11pm Fri & Sat). It's for gourmet housemade creams, served in a cup, cone or smashed between two freshly baked chocolate-chip cookies.

❼ Ercoles 1101

A funky counterpoint to the HD-inundated, design-heavy sports bars on Manhattan Beach Blvd. **Ercoles** (📞 310-372-1997; http://m.mainstreethub.com/ercoles1101#; 1101 Manhattan Ave; ⏰ 10am-2am) is a dark, chipped, well-irrigated hole with a barn door open to everyone from salty barflies to yuppie pub crawlers to volleyball stars.

Explore

Downtown

Take Manhattan, add a splash of Mexico City, a dash of Tokyo and Guangzhou, shake and pour. Your drink: Downtown LA. Rapidly evolving, 'DTLA' is the city's most intriguing patch, where cutting-edge architecture and world-class modern-art museums contrast sharply against blaring mariachi tunes, Chinese grocers, abject poverty and many of the city's hottest restaurants, bars, galleries and boutiques.

The Sights in a Day

☼ Have breakfast among the gourmet food stalls of the **Grand Central Market** (p121) before meandering down Broadway past the old theaters to the **Fashion District**, where even if there isn't a sample sale on you can explore the **California Market Center** (p123) and absorb the general fashionista vibe. Hit the epic **Grammy Museum** (p126) before heading north.

☼ Grab lunch at **Q Sushi** (p129) before strolling north past Pershing Square and into the Financial District. From here it's an easy walk two blocks north to the **Walt Disney Concert Hall** (p120), where you can catch the last tour of the day. Then walk down the road to the **MOCA Grand** (p126) and the **Broad** (p126).

☾ If it's a summer Friday night, you can start your evening with free **live music** (p134) at the California Plaza. Otherwise, head to the **Ace Hotel rooftop** (p133) for a sundowner, then to **Maccheroni Republic** (p130) for dinner and over to **Clifton's Republic** (p132) for a cocktail.

For a local's day in Downtown, see p122.

 Top Sight

Walt Disney Concert Hall (p120)

Local Life

The Fashion District (p122)

🖤 **Best of Los Angeles**

Eating
Otium (p121)

Cole's (p130)

Drinking
Upstairs at the Ace Hotel (p133)

New Jalisco Bar (p132)

Getting There

Ⓜ **Metro** Red Line trains run to Silver Lake, Hollywood and Universal Studios; Gold Line to Pasadena; Expo Line to Exposition Park, Culver City and Santa Monica; and Blue Line to Long Beach.

🚌 **Bus** Metro buses connect Downtown to most corners of the city. The LAX Flyaway (p179) shuttle departs from Union Station.

Top Sights
Walt Disney Concert Hall

A molten blend of steel, music and psychedelic architecture, this iconic concert venue is the home base of the Los Angeles Philharmonic, but has also hosted contemporary bands such as Phoenix and classic jazz men such as Sonny Rollins. Frank Gehry pulled out all the stops: the building is a gravity-defying sculpture of heaving and billowing stainless steel.

👁 Map p124, E2

📞 323-850-2000

www.laphil.org

111 S Grand Ave

admission free

🕑 guided tours usually noon & 1:15pm Thu-Sat, 10am & 11am Sun

Los Angeles Philharmonic

The only way to experience the auditorium is to see a show. The world-class **LA Phil** (☏323-850-2000; www.laphil.org; 111 S Grand Ave) performs classics and cutting-edge works at the Walt Disney Concert Hall, under the baton of Venezuelan phenom Gustavo Dudamel. In contrast to the exterior, the auditorium feels like the inside of a finely crafted cello, clad in walls of smooth Douglas fir with terraced 'vineyard' seating wrapped around a central stage. Even seats below the giant pipe organ offer excellent sight lines.

Redcat

Redcat (☏213-237-2800; www.redcat.org; 631 W 2nd St) is Downtown's most avant-garde performance laboratory where theater, dance, music, poetry and film merge into impressive exhibitions presented in its own theater and gallery within the Walt Disney Concert Hall complex. The curious name is an acronym for Roy and Edna Disney/Cal Arts Theater. Admission to the gallery (noon to 6pm Tuesday to Sunday) is free. Theater ticket prices vary.

Pipe Organ

The stunning pipe organ, a gift to LA county from the Toyota Corporation, incorporates 6134 pipes and took over 2000 hours to tune. The longest pipe is more than 32ft long and weighs upwards of 800 lbs. Shipped by sea from Germany, the instrument's total weight is over 40 metric tons. And it sounds just that big.

☑ Top Tips

▶ Free, self-guided audio tours are available most days and there are one-hour guided tours available too.

▶ Always check the website for tour times.

▶ Tours do not include a glimpse at the auditorium.

✕ Take a Break

In a nearby pavilion, **Otium** (☏213-935-8500; http://otiumla.com; 222 S Hope St, Downtown; dishes $15-45; ⏱11:30am-2:30pm & 5:30-10pm Tue-Thu, 11:30am-2:30pm & 5:30-11pm Fri, 11am-2:30pm & 5:30-11pm Sat, 11am-2:30pm & 5:30-10pm Sun; 🖥) is a standout Downtown eatery serving seasonal, modern American plates and inventive cocktails. For a cheaper (no less tasty) bite, the **Grand Central Market** (www.grandcentralmarket.com; 317 S Broadway; ⏱8am-10pm; Ⓜ Red/Purple Lines to Pershing Sq) is a 700yd walk away.

Local Life
The Fashion District

Bargain hunters love the frantic, 100-block warren of fashion in southwestern Downtown that is the Fashion District. Deals can be amazing, but first timers are often bewildered by the district's size and immense selection. For orientation, check out www.fashion district.org. Shops are generally open from 10am to 5pm daily, with Saturday being the busiest day because that's when many whole-salers open up to the public.

1 Back to School

The **Fashion Institute of Design and Merchandising** (213-623-5821; http://fidmmuseum.org; 919 S Grand Ave; admission free; ⏰10am-5pm Tue-Sat during exhibits; MRed/Purple/Blue/Expo Lines to 7th St/Metro Center) is a private college with an international student body. Very much part of the nearby Fashion District's soul, its gallery serves up some interesting rotating exhibits. Check the website to see what's on when.

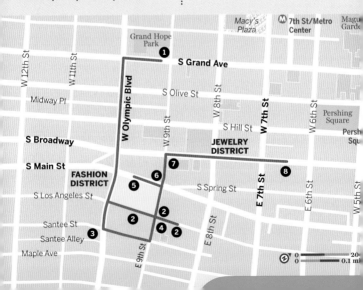

② Sample Sales

Sample sales are usually held on the last Friday of every month, with popular showrooms including the **Cooper Design Space** (📞213-627-3754; www.cooperdesignspace.com; 860 S Los Angeles St), **New Mart** (📞213-627-0671; www.newmart.net; 127 E 9th St) and the **Gerry Building** (www.gerrybuilding.com; 910 S Los Angeles St).

③ Bargain District

An actual alley, **Santee Alley** (www.thesanteealley.com; cnr Santee & 12th Sts; ⏱9:30am-6pm) is open every day and packed with solid bargains spanning everything from on-trend threads and kitschy gowns, to kicks, bling, eyewear, perfumes and more.

④ Quick Fix

Need that quick fix to sate you through the sample-sale madness? Head to the **Market** (📞213-488-9119; www.marketrestaurants.com; 862 S Los Angeles St; dishes $6-14; ⏱8am-4pm Mon-Fri; 📶🍴) for a pressed Cuban sandwich (citrus-glazed pork, ham and manchego) or a grilled ahi and seaweed salad. Save room for cupcakes.

⑤ The Hub

Although it's no longer the hippest building in the district, the **California Market Center** (📞213-630-3600; www.californiamarketcenter.com; 110 E 9th St) remains its axis, and is a venue for Fashion District sample sales. Check the website for upcoming sales and bring your own bags and plenty of cash (most vendors don't accept cards).

⑥ Clink of the Glass

A popular Fashion District well, **Pattern Bar** (📞213-627-7774; www.patternbar.com; 100 W 9th St; ⏱noon-10pm Sun-Wed, to midnight Thu, to 2am Fri & Sat; 📶) is a retro-spirited watering hole with twirling ceiling fans, parlor floors and cocktails celebrating its address. Chat hemlines and fabrics over tequila-fueled Chanels or gin-pimped McQueens, or butch it up with craft brews from as far afield as Iceland.

⑦ Theater

Currently the most active of Broadway's historic theaters, the **Orpheum** (📞877-677-4386; www.laorpheum.com; 842 S Broadway) hosts everything from touring musicals and rock bands to comedy shows and galas. A truly sumptuous place, its French baroque style is accented with silk tapestries, a gilded, coffered ceiling, an old brass box office and a still-functioning Wurlitzer organ that can replicate over 1400 orchestral sounds. See a show here if you can.

⑧ Art for the People

A mad swirl of art lovers invades Downtown once a month for liberally lubricated **Downtown Art Walks** (www.downtownartwalk.org; tickets $20-25; ⏱6-8pm 2nd Thu of month) that link more than 40 galleries and museums across the Downtown grid. You'll find most between 3rd and 9th and Broadway and Main.

Georgia St

Chick Hearn Ct

Pasadena Fwy

23

Grammy Museum
3

Cottage Pl

Francisco St

S Figueroa St

9

S Flower St

7th St/Metro Center

ARCO Plaza
17

W 12th St

S Hope St

SOUTH PARK

Macy's Plaza

Maguire Gardens

Bank
Amer
Plaza

W 11th St

Grand Hope Park

US Bank Tower
7

S Grand Ave

S Olive St

S Grand Ave

11

10

FINANCIAL DISTRICT

Midway Pl

21

W Olympic Blvd

W 9th St

W 8th St

25

S Hill St

26

20

W 6th St

Pershing Square

Pershing Square

S Broadway

JEWELRY DISTRICT

W 5th St

S Main St

18

S Broadway

W 4th St

S Los Angeles St

California Market Center

29

S Spring St

Harlem Pl

13

Santee St

FASHION DISTRICT

S Main St

16

Harlem Pl

E 11th St

E 9th St

E 8th St

E 7th St

14

E 6th St

E 5th St

E 4th St

Maple Ave

Wall St

E Olympic Blvd

Flower Market

Winston St

San Julian St

San Julian St

S San Pedro St

Agatha St

Crocker St

Towne Ave

ARTS DISTRICT

Stanford Ave

E   F   G   H

1

2

3

4

5

0   1 km
0   0.5 miles

Beverly Blvd

N Beaudry Ave

W Temple St

Pasadena Fwy

College St

W 1st St

N Figueroa St

Santa Ana Fwy

W Cesar E Chavez Ave

Alpine St

Hope St
Broad

**Walt Disney
Concert
Hall**

1

2

OCA Grand
S Olive St

N Grand Ave

Yale St

Alpine
Park

W College St

Civic Center/
Grand Park

Civic
Center

W Temple St

CHINATOWN

N Hill St

N Broadway

Chinatown

N Broadway

N Spring St

Arcadia St

Ord St

N Spring St

N Alameda St

4
City Hall

N Main St

N Main St

E 2nd St

N Los Angeles St

El Pueblo
de Los
Angeles

Union
Station

TLE
KYO

24

8

Amtrak

Judge John Aiso St

Union Station/
Gateway Transit
Center

Japanese
Village
Plaza

6

Japanese American
National Museum

Metrolink
Station

E Cesar E Chavez Ave

N Vignes St

Alameda St

E 1st St

E Temple St

Santa Ana Fwy

N Vignes St

28

5

Hauser
& Wirth

Sights

Broad
MUSEUM

1 ◎ Map p124, E2

From the instant it opened in September 2015, the Broad (rhymes with 'road') became a must-visit for contemporary-art fans. It houses the world-class collection of local philanthropist and billionaire real-estate honcho Eli Broad and his wife Edythe, with more than 2000 postwar pieces by dozens of heavy hitters, including Cindy Sherman, Jeff Koons, Andy Warhol, Roy Lichtenstein, Robert Rauschenberg, Keith Haring and Kara Walker. (☑213-232-6200; www.thebroad.org; 221 S Grand Ave; admission free; ⏰11am-5pm Tue & Wed, to 8pm Thu & Fri, 10am-8pm Sat, to 6pm Sun; P ♿; M Red/Purple Lines to Civic Center/Grand Park)

MOCA Grand
MUSEUM

2 ◎ Map p124, E2

MOCA's superlative art collection focuses mainly on works created from the 1940s to the present. There's no shortage of luminaries, among them Mark Rothko, Dan Flavin, Willem de Kooning, Joseph Cornell and David Hockney, their creations housed in a postmodern building by award-winning Japanese architect Arata Isozaki. Galleries are below ground, yet sky-lit bright. MOCA's other Downtown location, **MOCA Geffen** (☑213-625-4390; 152 N Central Ave; adult/student/child under 12yr $15/8/free, 5-8pm Thu free; ⏰11am-6pm Mon, Wed & Fri, to 8pm Thu, to 5pm Sat & Sun; M Gold Line to Little Tokyo/Arts District), focuses on more experimental, cutting-edge and conceptual works. (Museum of Contemporary Art; ☑213-626-6222; www.moca.org; 250 S Grand Ave; adult/child $15/free, 5-8pm Thu free; ⏰11am-6pm Mon, Wed & Fri, to 8pm Thu, to 5pm Sat & Sun)

Grammy Museum
MUSEUM

3 ◎ Map p124, A1

It's the highlight of **LA Live** (☑866-548-3452, 213-763-5483; www.lalive.com; 800 W Olympic Blvd; P ♿). Music lovers will get lost in interactive exhibits, which define, differentiate and link musical genres. Spanning three levels, the museum's rotating exhibitions might include threads worn by the likes of Michael Jackson, Whitney Houston and Beyonce, scribbled words from the hands of Count Basie and Taylor Swift and instruments once used by world-renowned rock deities. Inspired? Interactive sound chambers allow you to try your own hand at singing, mixing and remixing. (☑213-765-6800; www.grammymuseum.org; 800 W Olympic Blvd; adult/child $13/11; ⏰10:30am-6:30pm Mon-Fri, from 10am Sat & Sun; P ♿)

City Hall
LANDMARK

4 ◎ Map p124, F3

Until 1966 no LA building stood taller than the 1928 City Hall, which appeared in the *Superman* TV series and 1953 sci-fi thriller *War of the Worlds*. On clear days you'll have views of the city, the mountains and several dec-

City Hall

ades of Downtown growth from the observation deck. On the way up, stop off on level three to eye up City Hall's original main entrance, which features a breathtaking, Byzantine-inspired rotunda graced with marble flooring and a mosaic dome. (📞213-485-2121; www.lacity.org; 200 N Spring St; admission free; 🕙9am-5pm Mon-Fri)

Hauser & Wirth   GALLERY

5 ◎ Map p124, E5

The LA outpost of internationally acclaimed gallery Hauser & Wirth has art fiends in a flurry with its museum-standard exhibits of modern and contemporary art. It's a huge space, occupying 116,000 square feet of a

converted flour mill complex in the Arts District. Past exhibits have showcased the work of luminaries such as Louise Bourgeois, Eva Hesse and Jason Rhoades. The complex is also home to a superlative art book shop. (📞213-943-1620; www.hauserwirthlosangeles.com; 901 E 3rd St; admission free; 🕙11am-6pm Wed & Fri-Sun, to 8pm Thu)

Japanese American National Museum   MUSEUM

6 ◎ Map p124, E4

A great first stop in Little Tokyo, this is the country's first museum dedicated to the Japanese immigrant experience. The 2nd floor is home to the permanent 'Common

Ground' exhibition, which explores the evolution of Japanese-American culture since the late 19th century and offers moving insight into the painful chapter of America's WWII internment camps. Afterwards relax in the tranquil garden and browse the well-stocked gift shop. (☎ 213-625-0414; www.janm.org; 100 N Central Ave; adult/child $10/6, 5-8pm Thu & all day 3rd Thu of month free; ☺11am-5pm Tue, Wed & Fri-Sun, noon-8pm Thu; 🚻; Ⓜ Gold Line to Little Tokyo/Arts District)

US Bank Tower
LANDMARK

7 ◎ Map p124, D2

Although the spire-topped 73-story Wilshire Grand Tower is technically LA's tallest building by architectural height, the 1018ft US Bank Tower remains the city's tallest building to roof height. Destroyed by aliens in *Independence Day* and by a mega-quake in *San Andreas,* the skyscraper is home to the **OUE Skyspace LA** (☎ 213-894-9000; https://oue-skyspace.com; adult/senior/child $25/22/19; ☺10am-9pm Sun-Thu, to 10pm Fri & Sat; 🚻), a multilevel observation deck offering a spectacular 360-degree view of the city, hills, ocean and (in winter) snowcapped mountains. For an extra $8, visitors can experience the Skyslide, a see-through outdoor slide connecting the two observation-deck floors – a short, somewhat underwhelming 'thrill'. (633 W 5th St; Ⓜ Red/Purple Lines to Pershing Sq)

Union Station
NOTABLE BUILDING

8 ◎ Map p124, G4

Built on the site of LA's original Chinatown, Union Station opened in 1939 as America's last grand rail station. It's a glamorous exercise in Mission Revival style with art deco and American Indian accents. The marble-floored main hall, with cathedral ceilings, original leather chairs and 3000-pound chandeliers, is breathtaking. The station's Traxx Bar was once the telephone

Local Life
El Pueblo de Los Ángeles Historical Monument

A short stroll northwest of Union Station, this compact, colorful **district** (☎ 213-628-1274; www.elpueblo.lacity.org; Olvera St; admission free; ☺tours 10am, 11am & noon Tue-Sat; 🚻; Ⓜ Red/Purple/Gold Lines to Union Station), located near the spot where LA's first colonists settled in 1781, harbors the city's oldest buildings. Grab a map at the visitor center inside **Avila Adobe** (☎ 213-628-1274; www.elpueblo.lacity.org; 10 Olvera St; admission free; ☺9am-4pm) then wander through narrow **Olvera St**'s vibrant Mexican-themed stalls. Then visit **La Plaza** (La Plaza de Cultura y Artes; ☎ 213-542-6200; www.lapca.org; 501 N Main St; admission free; ☺noon-5pm Mon, Wed & Thu, to 6pm Fri-Sun; 🚻), a museum of the Mexican-American experience, and **La Placita** (www.laplacita.org; 535 N Main St; ☺6am-8:30pm), the original 1781 church.

room, complete with operator to place customers' calls. (www.amtrak.com; 800 N Alameda St; P)

Eating

Broken Spanish   MEXICAN $$$

9 ✗ Map p124, A2

Despite retro design nods such as concrete blocks, macrame plant hangers and terracotta lampshades, Ray Garcia's sleek Downtown eatery is all about confident, contemporary Mexican cooking. From the *chochoyotes* (masa dumplings with green garlic and pasilla pepper) to a rich, intense dish of mushrooms with black garlic, flavors are clean and intriguing, and the presentation polished. (☎213-749-1460; http://brokenspanish.com; 1050 S Flower St; mains $22-49; ⊙5:30-10pm Sun-Thu, to 11pm Fri & Sat; 🛜)

Q Sushi   SUSHI $$$

10 ✗ Map p124, C2

Sushi and sashimi hit dizzying highs at this *omakase* heavyweight, where bite-sized bliss comes from the likes of tender octopus braised in sake and brown sugar, or blow-torched toro made with rice fermented for a month. Dinner consists of 20 courses (lunch about half that), all created by Japanese sushi savant Hiro Naruke, who lost his business in the post-tsunami aftermath. Reserve ahead. (☎213-225-6285; www.qsushila.com; 521 W 7th St; per person lunch/dinner from $75/165; ⊙noon-1:30pm Tue-Fri, 6-9pm Tue-Sat; P)

Bottega Louie   ITALIAN $$

11 ✗ Map p124, C2

Divided into a patisserie, bar and dining room, this sprawling, loft-like space recalls the grand cafes of northern Italy: dapper barkeeps pour Aperol spritzers, waiters carry trays high and confidently, and a democratic mix of couples, suits and tourists tuck into decent bistro fare (go for the giant, Neapolitan-style pizzas). The macarons here are famous, though, frankly, we've had better elsewhere. (☎213-802-1470; www.bottegalouie.com; 700 S Grand Ave; pizzas $22, dishes $12-36; ⊙6:30am-11pm Mon-Thu, to midnight Fri, 8am-midnight Sat, 8am-11pm Sun; 🛜; MRed/Purple Lines to 7th St/Metro Center)

Sushi Gen   JAPANESE $$$

12 ✗ Map p124, E5

Come early to grab a table at this classic sushi spot, where bantering Japanese chefs carve thick slabs of melt-in-your-mouth salmon, buttery toro, Japanese snapper and more. At lunch, perch yourself at the sushi counter for a-la-carte options, or queue for a table in the dining room, where the sashimi lunch special ($17) is a steal. (☎213-617-0552; www.sushigen.org; 422 E 2nd St; sushi $11-23; ⊙11:15am-2pm & 5:30-9:45pm Tue-Fri, 5-9:45pm Sat; P; MGold Line to Little Tokyo/Arts District)

71 Above   MODERN AMERICAN $$$

Reserve ahead for a window table at fine-dining 71 Above (see 7 ✗ Map p124, D2), perched 950ft above Downtown streets. While it's difficult to upstage the views, chef Vartan Abgaryan offers strong competition with his creative, globally influenced flavors. Scan the skyline over dishes such as beets with chocolate wheat berries and blood orange, or lobster with Vadouvan curry, coconut, almond and barrel-aged fish sauce. (☎213-712-2683; www.71above.com; 633 W 5th St; 2-course set lunch $35, 3-course set dinner $70; ⏱11:30am-11pm Mon-Thu, to midnight Fri, 5pm-midnight Sat, 5-10pm Sun; P; MRed/Purple Lines to Pershing Sq)

Maccheroni Republic   ITALIAN $$

13 ⊗ Map p124, D3

Tucked away on a still ungentrified corner is this gem with a leafy heated patio and tremendous Italian slow-cooked food. Don't miss the *polpettine di gamberi* (flattened ground shrimp cakes fried in olive oil) and its range of delicious house-made pastas. Perfectly al dente, the pasta is made using organic semolina flour and served with gorgeous crusty bread to mop up the sauce. (☎213-346-9725; www.maccheronirepublic.com; 332 S Broadway; mains $11-18; ⏱11:30am-2:30pm & 5:30-10pm Mon-Thu, 11:30am-2:30pm & 5:30-10:30pm Fri, 11:30am-10:30pm Sat, 11:30am-9pm Sun)

Cole's   SANDWICHES $

14 ⊗ Map p124, C3

An atmospheric old basement tavern with vintage vinyl booths, original glass lighting and historic photos, Cole's is known for originating the French Dip sandwich way back in 1908, when those things cost a nickel. You know the drill – French bread piled with sliced lamb, beef, turkey, pork or pastrami, dipped once or twice in *au jus*. (☎213-622-4090; http://213hospitality.com/project/coles; 118 E 6th St; sandwiches $10-13.50; ⏱11am-midnight Sun-Wed, to 2am Thu-Sat; 🛜)

Little Sister   SOUTHEAST ASIAN $$

San Gabriel Valley–born-and-bred chef Tin Vuong has broken the mold with this modern Singaporean-style, pan-Asian bistro (see 10 ⊗ Map p124, C2). The ever-changing share-plate menu boasts rice paper rolls, salads, meat and poultry, noodles, banh mi and congee, and veggies really excel, such as cold *ma po doufu* (tofu in hot chili–broad bean paste), Myanmar okra curry and XO pea tendrils with dried scallop shards. (☎213-628-3146; www.littlesisterla.com; 523 W 7th St; dishes $8-28; 🚌Metro bus 20, 720, MRed, Blue & Expo Lines to 7th St/Metro Center)

Madcapra   MIDDLE EASTERN $

This hectic stall (see 15 ⊗ Map p124, D3) peddles flawless falafel sandwiches. The flatbread is rolled and grilled fresh, then filled with pillowy falafel with just the right amount of crunch. Choose from four color-coded sandwiches (the 'red' is the most popular), all of which can also be made as a salad. Pair with an iced cardamom coffee or *shandria* (ginger lemonade, beer and fruit). (☎213-357-2412; www.madcapra.com; Grand Central Market, 317 S Broadway; salads & sandwiches $11-13;

Dish at Orsa & Winston

⊙11am-5pm Sun-Wed, to 9pm Thu-Sat;
Ⓜ Red/Purple Lines to Pershing Sq)

Eggslut
DINER $

 15 Map p124, D3

A classic breakfast counter has been brought back to life by local foodie punks who, among other things, stuff house-made turkey sausage, eggs and mustard aioli in brioche, and make a dish known only as 'the slut': a coddled egg nestled on top of potato puree poached in a glass jar and served with sliced baguette. To avoid the queues, head in around 9am Monday to Wednesday. (www.eggslut.com; Grand Central Market, 317 S Broadway; dishes $6-9; ⊙8am-4pm)

Orsa & Winston
FUSION $$$

 16 Map p124, D3

Progressive, well-executed Italo-Asian fusion rules the roost here. Grain bowls feature on the simpler lunch menu – choose your base (quinoa, barley, farro or rice), your flavor (anything from curry to seafood crudo) and any sides. Dinner is a fancier *omakase* affair, its six-course adventures featuring concoctions such as cultured-grain agnolotti paired with *paitan* broth, geoduck clams, *tatsoi* (Asian greens) and pecorino sardo. (☎213-687-0300; www.orsaandwinston.com; 122 W 4th St; lunch bowls $10-14, 6-course dinner tasting menu $85; ⊙noon-2pm Tue-Fri, 6-11pm Tue-Sat; Ⓜ Red/Purple Lines to Pershing Sq)

Lemonade

CALIFORNIAN $

 17 Map p124, D2

In the basement food hall of City National Plaza, trendy Lemonade offers the Cafeteria 2.0 experience – counter slop ditched for superfresh gourmet grub. There are six food stations – Market Place, Leafy Greens, Land and Sea, Sandwiches, Hot Dishes and Dessert – serving up the likes of watermelon radish and seared ahi tuna salad, and Thai-inspired pineapple chicken with crisp beans and toasted coconut. (213-488-0299; www.lemonadela.com; 505 S Flower St; meals $8-13; ⏰11am-3pm Mon-Fri; 🛜🖊; MRed/Purple Line to 7th St/Metro Center)

Drinking

Clifton's Republic

COCKTAIL BAR

 18 Map p124, C3

Opened in 1935 and back after a $10-million nip-and-tuck, multilevel mixed-crowd Clifton's defies descrip-

tion. You can chow retro-cafeteria classics (meals around $14.75) by a forest waterfall, order drinks from a Gothic church altar, watch burlesque performers shimmy in the shadow of a 40ft faux redwood, or slip through a glass-paneled door to a luxe tiki paradise where DJs spin in a repurposed speedboat. (213-627-1673; www.cliftonsla.com; 648 S Broadway; ⏰11am-midnight Tue-Thu, to 2am Fri, 10am-2:30am Sat, 10am-midnight Sun; 🛜; MRed/Purple Lines to Pershing Sq)

Edison

COCKTAIL BAR

 19 Map p124, E3

Accessed through easy-to-miss Harlem Pl alleyway, this extraordinary basement lounge sits in a century-old power plant. It's like a dimly lit, steampunk wonderland, punctuated with vintage generators, handsome leather lounges and secret nooks. Look for celebrity signatures in the original coal furnace and stick around for the live tunes (anything from jazz to folk), burlesque or aerialist performances.

(☑213-613-0000; www.edisondowntown.
com; 108 W 2nd St; ☺5pm-2am Wed-Fri, from
7pm Sat; Ⓜ Red/Purple Lines to Civic Center/
Grand Park)

Upstairs at the Ace Hotel   BAR

20 🚇 Map p124, B3

What's not to love about a rooftop
bar with knockout Downtown views,
powerful cocktails and a luxe, safari-
inspired fit-out? Perched on the 14th
floor of the Ace Hotel, this chilled, sophisticated space has on-point DJs and
specially commissioned artworks that
include an installation made using
Skid Row blankets. (www.acehotel.com/
losangeles; 929 S Broadway; ☺11am-2am)

Mikkeller DTLA   BEER HALL

21 🚇 Map p124, A2

This cool, influential Copenhagen import puts a contemporary spin on the
old beer hall. Fitted out with booths,
communal bar tables and cartoon
artwork by Philly-based artist Keith
Shore, the industrial loft peddles craft
beers from some of the world's most
interesting microbreweries. Look for
LA brewers such as Eagle Rock and
Mumford, as well as Mikkeller's own
renowned suds. (☑213-596-9005; www.
mikkellerbar.com/la; 330 W Olympic Blvd;
☺bar 5pm-midnight Sun-Wed, to 2am Thu-
Sat, cafe 8am-5pm daily)

Varnish   BAR

Tucked into the back of Cole's (p130)
is this cubby-hole-sized speakeasy
(see 14 ✖ Map p124, C3), where good live

jazz burns Sunday through Tuesday.
(☑213-817-5321; http://213hospitality.
com/the-varnish; 118 E 6th St; ☺7pm-2am;
Ⓜ Red/Purple Lines to Pershing Sq)

EightyTwo   BAR

22 🚇 Map p124, E5

Cocktails, pinball machines and arcade games make for oh-so-retro good
times at this graffiti-soaked warehouse
bar. Named for 1982 (the height of
the 'Arcade Age'), its 40-plus consoles
include classics Donkey Kong, Space
Invaders and Ms Pac-Man (with drink
coasters for grown-up '80s kids).
Nightly DJs and rotating food trucks
fuel the crowds. (☑213-626-8200; http://
eightytwo.la; 707 E 4th Pl; ☺6pm-2am Tue-
Thu, from 5pm Fri, from 2pm Sat & Sun)

Local Life
Music Center of Los Angeles County

The **Music Center** (www.music
center.org) is a touchstone of
performing arts in America. **Center
Theatre Group** produces works
that have gone on to win Tony and
Pulitzer Prizes. Venues include
Walt Disney Concert Hall (p120),
the **Ahmanson Theatre** (☑213-628-
2772; www.centertheatregroup.org; 135 N
Grand Ave), which stages large-scale
Broadway runs, and the intimate,
theater-in-the-round **Mark Taper
Forum** (☑213-628-2772; www.center
theatregroup.org; 135 N Grand Ave).
Showtimes vary by venue.

Entertainment

Staples Center
STADIUM

23 ⭐ Map p124, A1

This saucer-shaped sports and entertainment arena is home court for the Los Angeles **Lakers** (☎888-929-7849; www.nba.com/lakers; tickets from $30), **Clippers** (☎213-204-2900; www.nba.com/clippers; tickets from $20) and Sparks basketball teams, and home ice for the LA Kings. The stadium also hosts pop and rock concerts. (☎213-742-7100; www.staplescenter.com; 1111 S Figueroa St)

Blue Whale
JAZZ

24 ⭐ Map p124, E4

An intimate, concrete-floored space on the top floor of Weller Court in Little

Local Life
Last Bookstore in LA
It's not literally LA's **last bookstore** (☎213-488-0599; www.lastbookstorela.com; 453 S Spring St; ☺10am-10pm Mon-Thu, to 11pm Fri & Sat, to 9pm Sun), but it's a sight to be seen nonetheless. What started as a one-man operation out of a Main St storefront is now California's largest new-and-used bookstore, spanning two levels of an old bank building. Eye up the cabinets of rare books before heading upstairs, home to a horror-and-crime book den, a book tunnel and a few art galleries to boot. The store also houses a terrific vinyl collection.

Tokyo, Blue Whale serves top-notch jazz nightly from 9pm. The crowd is eclectic, the beers craft and the bar bites decent. Acts span emerging and edgy to established, and the acoustics are excellent. Note: bring cash for the cover charge. (☎213-620-0908; www.bluewhalemusic.com; 123 Onizuka St, Suite 301; cover $5-20; ☺8pm-2am, closed 1st Sun of month; Ⓜ Gold Line to Little Tokyo/Arts District)

Grand Performances
LIVE MUSIC

25 ⭐ Map p124, D2

Each summer non-profit Grand Performances presents a brilliant season of free outdoor concerts by the splashing fountains of California Plaza in Downtown LA. Offerings span classical music to hip-hop, world music and more, with both local and international talent in the mix. Check the website for details. (☎213-687-2190; www.grandperformances.org; California Plaza, 300 & 350 S Grand Ave; admission free; ☺Jun-Sep; Ⓜ Red/Purple Lines to Pershing Sq)

United Artists Theatre
LIVE MUSIC, DANCE

26 ⭐ Map p124, B3

A historic gem of a theater restored by the Ace Hotel, which curates the calendar. Offerings are eclectic, ranging from music performances to dance acts and film screenings. Recent events include the West Coast premiere of Tyler Hubby's documentary film *Tony Conrad: Completely in the Present,* with a post-screening conversation moderated by Henry Rollins. Check the website for what's on. (☎213-623-3233; www.acehotel.com/losangeles/theatre; 929 S Broadway)

Shopping

Raggedy Threads   VINTAGE

27 🔒 Map p124, E4

A tremendous vintage Americana store just off the main Little Tokyo strip. There's plenty of beautifully ragged denim, with a notable collection of pre-1950s workwear from the US, Japan and France. You'll also find a good number of Victorian dresses, soft T-shirts and a wonderful turquoise collection at decent prices. (☎213-620-1188; www.raggedythreads.com; 330 E 2nd St; ⊙noon-8pm Mon-Sat, to 6pm Sun; Ⓜ Gold Line to Little Tokyo/Arts District)

Apolis   FASHION & ACCESSORIES

28 🔒 Map p124, E5

A tremendous, but not cheap, menswear brand that creates tailored chinos, jeans, T-shirts and blazers. Owned by two Santa Barbarian brothers, the line fits comfortably between J Crew and James Perse. It's all about fair trade, and proves it with develop-ment projects in American inner cities, Peruvian and Ugandan villages and Bangladesh. (☎855-894-1559; www.apolisglobal.com; 806 E 3rd St; ⊙noon-6pm Mon-Wed, to 7pm Thu, 11am-7pm Fri & Sat, 11am-6pm Sun)

Poketo   BOUTIQUE

In the Arts District, this is Poketo's flagship store (see 28 🔒 Map p124, E5). Shop the shelves for a thoughtful mix of mainly US-designed lifestyle products, from hand-poured scented candles and beauty products, to hand-painted ceramics, jewelry, bags and super-cool textiles. (☎213-537-0751; www.poketo.com; 820 E 3rd St; ⊙noon-7pm Mon, from 11am Tue-Sun)

Hive   ART

29 🔒 Map p124, C3

Nestled in a gentrifying stretch of Spring is this seemingly small, but surprisingly deep, artist-owned gallery, where the creative output focuses on pop surrealism. If you're around on the first Saturday of the month, head in for its rocking openings, complete with live performances and an eclectic Downtown crowd. (☎213-955-9051; www.thehivegallery.com; 729 S Spring St; ⊙1-6pm Wed-Sat)

Top Sights
Exposition Park

Getting There

🚇 10 minutes from Downtown LA on the Metro Expo Line. The same train continues to Santa Monica.

🚗 Take the Vermont Ave exit off the I-10 Fwy.

A quick jaunt south of Downtown LA by Metro Expo Line or DASH bus, the family-friendly Exposition Park began as an agricultural fairground in 1872, then devolved into a magnet for the down-and-out and finally emerged as a patch of public greenery in 1913. The draws here are a trio of great museums and the Los Angeles Memorial Stadium, where the USC Trojans play (American) football.

California Science Center

700 Exposition Park Dr

P ♿

California Science Center

Top billing at the **Science Center** (🎬 film schedule 213-744-2019, info 323-724-3623; www.californiasciencecenter.org; IMAX movie adult/child $8.50/5.25; ⏰10am-5pm) goes to the Space Shuttle Endeavour, one of only four space shuttles nationwide, and there's plenty else to see at this museum dedicated to space, creativity, the human body, ecosystems and more.

Natural History Museum

Dinos to diamonds, bears to beetles, hissing roaches to African elephants – this **museum** (📞213-763-3466; www.nhm.org; adult/student & senior/child $12/9/5; ⏰9:30am-5pm) will take you around the world and back, through millions of years in time. It's all housed in a beautiful 1913 Spanish Renaissance–style building that stood in for Columbia University in the first Toby McGuire *Spider-Man* movie.

California African American Museum

CAAM (📞213-744-7432; www.caamuseum.org; 600 State Dr; admission free; ⏰10am-5pm Tue-Sat, from 11am Sun) showcases African-American artists and the African-American experience, with a special focus on California and LA. Exhibits change a few times each year in galleries around a sunlit atrium.

Los Angeles Memorial Coliseum

Built in 1923, this grand **stadium** (📞213-741-0410; www.lacoliseum.com; 3911 S Figueroa St; guided/self-guided tours $25/10; ⏰self-guided tours 10am-4pm Wed-Sun, guided tours 10:30am & 1:30pm Wed-Sun) hosted the 1932 and 1984 Summer Olympic Games, the 1959 baseball World Series and two Super Bowls, and it's the temporary home stadium for the Los Angeles Rams and permanent home of University of Southern California Trojans (American) football teams. Informative guided tours dish the history and take you inside locker rooms, press box, the field and more.

☑ Top Tips

▶ Roam the Natural History Museum at night on First Fridays when the hipsters, and some families, invade for a lineup of live music and stellar DJs.

▶ When the butterfly and spider pavilions are up, buy tickets in advance to ensure entry.

✗ Take a Break

For a blast of African-American culture, head to **Leimert Park** (Degnan Blvd & 43rd St), the community's cultural hub, where you can sample Caribbean cuisine, catch live jazz and peruse Pan-African handicrafts.

Local Life
Pasadena

Getting There

Ⓜ Metrolink's Gold Line serves Pasadena and connects it to downtown.

🚗 Take I-110 from downtown or the I-134 from Burbank.

One could argue that there is more blue-blood, meat-eating, robust Americana in Pasadena than in all other LA neighborhoods combined. Here is a community with a preppy old soul, a historical perspective, an appreciation for art and jazz and a slightly progressive undercurrent.

❶ Circumnavigate the Rose Bowl

One of LA's most venerable landmarks, the 1922 **Rose Bowl Stadium** (☎626-577-3100; www.rosebowlstadium. com; 1001 Rose Bowl Dr) can seat up to 93,000 spectators and has its moment in the sun every New Year's Day when it hosts the famous Rose Bowl postseason college football game. It is surrounded by Brookside Park, which is a nice spot for hiking, cycling and picnicking. Many locals run or pedal around the stadium each afternoon.

❷ Tour the Gamble House

It's the exquisite attention to detail that impresses most at the **Gamble House** (☎info 626-793-3334, tickets 844-325-0712; www.gamblehouse.org; 4 Westmoreland Pl, Pasadena; tours adult/child $15/free; ⏰tours 11:30am-3pm Thu & Fri, noon-3pm Sat & Sun Sep-May, 11am-3pm Thu-Sat, noon-3pm Sun Jun-Aug, bookstore 11am-2pm Tue, 10am-5pm Thu-Sun; **P**), a 1908 masterpiece of Craftsman architecture built by Charles and Henry Greene for Proctor & Gamble heir David Gamble.

❸ Enjoy World-class Art

Rodin's *The Thinker* is only a mind-teasing overture to the full symphony of art in store at this exquisite museum. The highly accessible, user-friendly galleries at **Norton Simon** (www.nortonsimon.org; 411 W Colorado Blvd, Pasadena; adult/child $12/free; ⏰noon-5pm Mon, Wed & Thu, 11am-8pm Fri & Sat, 11am-5pm Sun; **P**) teem with choice works by Rembrandt, Renoir, Raphael, Van Gogh, Botticelli and Picasso.

❹ A Steampunk Scene

An amazing boutique with a steampunk vibe, **Gold Bug** (☎626-744-9963; www.goldbugpasadena.com; 22 E Union St, Pasadena; ⏰10am-5pm Mon, to 6pm Tue-Sat, noon-5pm Sun) shows work and collections created or curated by 100 area artists. We saw one robotic metallic Cheshire Cat, exquisite vintage jewelry and lamps, raw crystals and selenite and a terrific art-book collection.

❺ California Style

The **Pasadena Museum of California Art** (☎626-568-3665; www.pmcaonline. org; 490 E Union St, Pasadena; adult/student & senior/child $7/5/free; 1st Fri & 3rd Thu of month free; ⏰noon-5pm Wed-Sun, to 8pm 3rd Thu each month; **P**) is a progressive gallery dedicated to art, architecture and design created by California artists since 1850. Shows change every few months. The museum is free on the first Friday of every month.

❻ Dinner & Music

Dine on acclaimed Basque cuisine at the chef-owned **Racion** (☎626-396-3090; www.racionrestaurant.com; 119 W Green St, Pasadena; small plates $4-14, mains $20-58; ⏰6-10pm Mon-Thu, 11:30am-3pm & 6-10:30pm Fri, 11:30am-3pm & 5:30-10:30pm Sat, 5:30-10pm Sun), then enjoy some of the best LA-area jazz talent doing their thing in **Red White & Bluezz**' brassy Old Town environs. The latter also serves dinner.

Explore

Burbank & Universal City

Home to most of LA's major movie studios – including Warner Bros, Disney and Universal – the sprawling grid of suburbia known as 'the Valley' is where the real folk live, making it more laid-back and down to earth than other areas in the city.

The Sights in a Day

☀ Breakfast at **Bob's Big Boy** (p147), Burbank's original drive-in diner, before heading over to **Warner Bros** (p146) for a working studio tour without the theme park attractions.

☀ Grab lunch among the producers, aspiring writers and actors at **Aroma** (p148), then take the family to **Universal Studios** (p142) for an afternoon and adventure in the **Wizarding World of Harry Potter**, or the **3-D Transformers** ride and the **Despicable Me Minion Mayhem**. If you've had your fill of the theme-park disco, blitz over to **It's a Wrap!** (p149) before closing time.

🌙 If it's a balmy evening, stroll **Universal CityWalk** (p143). Otherwise, head over to Sushi Row for dinner at the undercover heaven that is **Asanebo** (p146) before catching a jazz, rock or comedy show at **Vitello's** (p147).

👁 **Top Sight**

Universal Studios (p142)

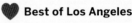 **Best of Los Angeles**

Eating
Bob's Big Boy (p147)

Shopping
It's a Wrap (p149)

Getting There

Ⓢ **Subway** Take the Metro Red subway line from Downtown LA and Hollywood to Universal City and the North Hollywood Stations.

Top Sights
Universal Studios

The magic of movie making gets its due at ever-popular Universal, one of the world's oldest continuously operating movie studios and theme parks, where thrill rides, live performances, interactive shows and back-lot tram tours perpetually draw the masses. Although it is a working studio the chances of seeing any action, let alone a star, are slim.

👁 Map p144, E5

📞 800-864-8377

www.universalstudioshollywood.com

100 Universal City Plaza, Universal City

admission from $99, child under 3yr free

🕐 daily, hours vary

The Simpsons rides

Wizarding World of Harry Potter

At Universal's biggest attraction (expect long queues), climb aboard the **Flight of the Hippogriff** roller coaster and the 3-D ride **Harry Potter and the Forbidden Journey**. Buy wizarding equipment and 'every-flavour' beans in the fantasy-themed shops then dig into a feast platter with frosty mugs of 'butterbeer' at Three Broomsticks restaurant.

Other Top Universal Attractions

Elsewhere in the park, the **Jurassic Park** ride is a gentle float through a prehistoric jungle with a rather 'raptor-ous' ending. **Revenge of the Mummy** is a short, but thrilling, indoor roller-coaster romp through 'Imhotep's Tomb' that at one point has you going backwards and hits speeds of up to 45mph. A ride based on **The Simpsons** sends guests rocketing along with the Simpson family to experience a side of Springfield previously unexplored.

Universal CityWalk

Flashing video screens, oversized facades and garish color combos (think Blade Runner meets Willy Wonka) animate **Universal CityWalk** (☎818-622-4455; www.citywalkhollywood.com; 100 Universal City Dr, Universal City; ⏲11am-9pm Mon-Thu, to 11pm Fri-Sun; ♿; ⓂUniversal City), the outdoor shopping concourse adjacent to Universal Studios. CityWalk's 65 shops, restaurants and entertainment venues offer a mix of mid- and lowbrow attractions, with low leading by a nose.

☑ Top Tips

▶ Try to budget a full day to see Universal, especially in summer.

▶ To beat the crowds, get there before the gates open or invest in the Front of Line Pass (from $199) or the deluxe guided VIP Experience (from $359).

▶ Buying online tickets usually yields discounts and coupons.

✗ Take a Break

There are plenty of dining choices at Universal CityWalk but we suggest heading to Ventura Blvd's Sushi Row, where you can splurge at Asanebo (p146) or have sneaky-good affordable fare at Daichan (p147).

For reviews see

◉	Top Sights	p142
◎	Sights	p146
✕	Eating	p146
☺	Drinking	p148
✦	Entertainment	p149
🔒	Shopping	p149

W Burbank B▶

Clean Ave

Vineland Ave

North Hollywood

Ⓜ Chandler Blvd

NORTH HOLLYWOOD

Weddington St

North Hollywood Park

14 ✦ Dundas Dr

W Magnolia Bl

Magnolia Blvd

Otsego St   3 ◎   Hartsook St

Bakman Ave

NoHo Arts District

Laurel Canyon Blvd

Colfax Ave

Lankershim Blvd

Clean Ave

Riverside Dr

Camarillo S

Ventura Fwy

Tujunga Ave

Hollywood Fwy

Riverside Dr

Hollywood Fwy

Lankershim Blvd

Moorpark St

8 ✕ ✕ 9

Colfax Ave

4

✕

7

Ventura Blvd

12

Arch Dr

✕ 5

11 ✕

Ventura Blvd

13

✕ 10

STUDIO CITY

Ⓝ 0 —————— 1 km
   0 —————— 0.5 miles

15 ✦

Laurel Canyon Blvd

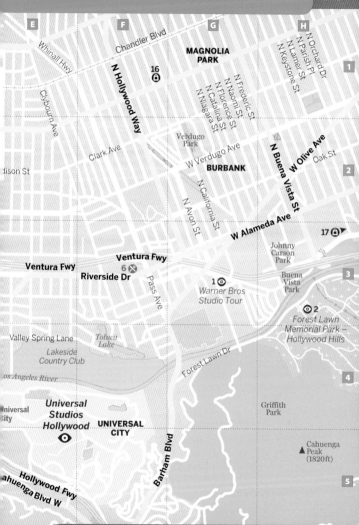

E

F

G

H

Whinall Hwy

Chandler Blvd

MAGNOLIA
PARK

N Orchard Dr
N Parish Pl
N Lamer St
N Keystone St

1

Clybourn Ave

N Hollywood Way

16

N Frederic St
N Naomi St
N Florence St
N Catalina St
N Niagara St

Verdugo
Park

N Buena Vista St

W Olive Ave

Oak St

Clark Ave

W Verdugo Ave

BURBANK

adison St

N California St

2

N Avon St

W Alameda Ave

17

Johnny
Carson
Park

Ventura Fwy

Ventura Fwy

6

Buena
Vista
Park

3

Riverside Dr

Pass Ave

1

Warner Bros
Studio Tour

2

Forest Lawn
Memorial Park –
Hollywood Hills

Valley Spring Lane

Toluca
Lake

Lakeside
Country Club

os Angeles River

Forest Lawn Dr

4

Universal
Studios
Hollywood

UNIVERSAL
CITY

Griffith
Park

niversal
City

Barham Blvd

Cahuenga
Peak
(1820ft)

5

Hollywood Fwy
ahuenga Blvd W

Sights

Warner Bros Studio Tour · TOUR

1 ◎ Map p144, G3

This tour offers the most fun, yet authentic, look behind the scenes of a major movie studio. The 2¼-hour romp kicks off with a video of WB's greatest film hits (*Rebel Without a Cause, Harry Potter* etc) before a tram whisks you around 110 acres of sound stages, back-lot sets and technical departments, including props, costumes and the paint shop, and a collection of Batmobiles. (☎877-492-8687, 818-972-8687; www.wbstudiotour.com; 3400 W Riverside Dr; tours adult/child 8-12yr from $62/52; ◎8:30am-3:30pm, extended hours Jun-Aug; ☐155, 222, 501 stop about 400yd from tour center)

Understand
Museum of Neon Art

Neon signage is a defining element of LA's cityscape, and the collection at this **museum** (☎818-696-2149; www.neonmona.org; 216 S Brand Blvd, Glendale; adult/student $10/8; ◎noon-7pm Thu-Sat, to 5pm Sun) east of Burbank includes signage from some of the region's best-known establishments, from the legendary (departed) Brown Derby to the Pep Boys auto-repair shops. MONA also holds twice-monthly 'Neon Cruises' on open-topped double-decker buses.

Forest Lawn Memorial Park – Hollywood Hills · CEMETERY

2 ◎ Map p144, H3

Pathos, art and patriotism rule at this humongous cemetery next to Griffith Park. A fine catalog of old-time celebrities, including Lucille Ball, Bette Davis and Stan Laurel, rests within the grounds strewn with paeans to early North American history. (www.forestlawn.com; 6300 Forest Lawn Dr; ◎8am-5pm; Ⓟ)

NoHo Arts District · NEIGHBORHOOD

3 ◎ Map p144, C2

North Hollywood (NoHo) was a down-on-its-heels neighborhood of artists, but thanks to redevelopment it now boasts some 20 stage theaters in 1 sq mile and a burgeoning community of galleries, restaurants and vintage-clothing stores around them. (www.nohoartsdistrict.com)

Eating

Asanebo · SUSHI $$$

4 ✕ Map p144, A4

Although it's in a strip mall (welcome to the Valley), Asanebo is a Sushi Row standout thanks to dishes such as halibut sashimi with fresh truffle, and *kanpachi* with miso and serrano chilies. Chef Tetsuya Nakao was one of the chefs who helped launch the Nobu Japanese restaurant empire. (☎818-760-3348; www.asanebo-restaurant.com; 11941 Ventura Blvd; dishes $3-21; ◎noon-2pm & 6-10:30pm Tue-Fri, 6-10:30pm Sat, to 10pm Sun; Ⓟ; ☐MTA lines 150, 240)

Daichan

JAPANESE $$

5  Map p144, C4

Tucked away in an unassuming mini-mall and stuffed with knickknacks, pasted with posters and staffed by a sunny, sweet owner-operator, this off-beat, home-style Japanese diner offers some of the best (and tastiest) deals on Sushi Row. Fried seaweed tofu *gyoza* are divine and so are the bowls – especially the *negitoro* bowl, which puts fatty tuna over rice, lettuce and seaweed. (☏818-980-8450; 11288 Ventura Blvd; mains $8-20; ⏱11:30am-3pm & 5:30-9pm Mon-Fri, noon-3pm & 5-9pm Sat; ⓟ)

Bob's Big Boy

DINER $

6  Map p144, F3

Bob, that cheeky, pompadoured kid in red-checkered pants, hasn't aged a lick since serving his first double-decker more than half a century ago. This Wayne McAllister–designed, Googie-style 1949 coffee shop is the oldest remaining Bob's Big Boy in America, serving a down-home menu centered on burgers, fries and chicken. (☏818-843-9334; www.bigboy.com; 4211 W Riverside Dr; burgers, sandwiches & salads $9-11.50, mains $9.50-14.50; ⏱24hr; ⓟ♿;🚌line 155 to Riverside Dr & Rose St)

Barrel & Ashes

BARBECUE $$

7  Map p144, B4

Barbecue with a pedigree; there's a concept. This stylish shop was founded by alumni of the Napa Valley's famed French Laundry and smokes

Forest Lawn Memorial Park – Hollywood Hills

meats such as beef brisket and pork spare ribs over California red oak. The 1940s building shows off original tile around contemporary communal tables, a sidewalk patio and a cool bar. (☏818-623-8883; www.barrelandashes.com; 11801 Ventura Blvd; mains $11-19; ⏱11am-3pm Mon-Fri, 5-10pm Sun-Thu, until 11pm Fri & Sat, 10:30am-3pm Sat & Sun; ⓟ)

Vitello's

ITALIAN $$

8  Map p144, C3

This sophisticated spot with brick and black-mottled walls has been in business since 1964 thanks to dishes such as chicken penne, branzino filet, plenty of pastas and hearty dinners like double-bone pork chops and American Wagyu flat iron steaks.

Aroma Coffee & Tea

This popular **cafe** (📞818-508-7377; www.aromacoffeeandtea.com; 4360 Tujunga Ave; ⊙6am-11pm Mon-Sat, from 6:30am Sun) is in a converted, artsy, multi room (yet somehow still cozy) house; outside, tables crowd leafy, heated patios and the line runs out the door. Coffees are great and the humongous menu (mains $11 to $15) includes goat-cheese-and-walnut salads, popular turkey burgers and breakfasts such as chilaquiles and breakfast enchiladas, or veggie Reuben and lobster club sandwiches.

Upstairs, the E-Spot supper club gigs in jazz, pop, rock and comedy (cover varies). There's even a new speakeasy. (📞818-769-0905; www.vitellosrestaurant.com; 4349 Tujunga Ave; mains lunch $12-24, dinner $17-32; ⊙11am-10pm Mon-Thu, to 11pm Fri, 10am-11pm Sat, 10am-10pm Sun; 🅿)

Caioti Pizza Cafe ITALIAN $$

 9 Map p144, C3

Once set in Laurel Canyon, this long-loved Italian cafe serves salads, bison burgers and Italian sausage sandwiches, as well as some terrific pizzas and pastas. But it's the 'The' Salad (romaine, watercress, walnuts and gorgonzola) that has become urban legend; some say it can induce labor in pregnant women. (📞818-761-3588; www.caiotipizzacafe.com; 4346 Tujunga Ave; mains $9-17; ⊙10am-10pm Mon-Thu, to 11pm Fri, 9am-11pm Sat, to 10:30pm Sun)

Kazu Sushi JAPANESE $$$

10 Map p144, C4

Stuck in a cramped and otherwise nondescript split-level mini-mall that's easy to miss is one of the best-kept secrets among LA's sushi aficionados. Kazu Sushi is Michelin-rated, very high-end, has a terrific sake selection and is worth the splurge on the *omakase* course. (📞818-763-4836; 11440 Ventura Blvd; dishes $10-19; ⊙noon-2pm & 6-9:45pm Mon-Fri, 6-9:45pm Sat; 🅿)

Drinking

Firefly LOUNGE

11 Map p144, B4

The bar at this restaurant has the sexiest library this side of an Anne Rice novel – bordello-red lighting, low-slung couches and flickering candles, all surrounded by shelves of somber-looking tomes. Not that anyone's opened one – the members of this upwardly mobile crowd are too busy reading each other. (📞818-762-1833; www.fireflystudiocity.com; 11720 Ventura Blvd; ⊙5pm-2am Mon-Sat, 11am-3pm & 5pm-1am Sun; 🚇MTA lines 150, 240)

Laurel Tavern PUB

 12 Map p144, A4

This new, tastefully modern pub with wood floors, wood-slab bar and brick walls has an extensive craftsman beer and wine list on the chalkboard. It has sports on the TV, enticing pub grub and a full bar, and there's a covered sidewalk terrace to enjoy the weather. (www.laureltavern.com; 11938 Ventura Blvd; ⏱noon-1am; 🚌MTA lines 150, 240)

Oil Can Harry's   GAY

13 🚇 Map p144, B4

The Valley's gay bar of record (since 1968) is a little bit country and a little bit rock and roll, with disco, salsa and lounge thrown in. The lineup on the main dance floor includes country Tuesday and Friday nights, Latin Thursdays and retro-disco Saturdays, while the upstairs loft offers happy hours, karaoke and piano singers. (☎818-760-9749; www.oilcanharrysla.com; 11502 Ventura Blvd; 🚌MTA lines 150, 240)

Entertainment

El Portal   THEATER

14 ⭐ Map p144, C1

The stage of this one-time vaudeville house from 1926 has been graced by headliners from Debbie Reynolds to Smokey Robinson, Carol Channing to James Corden. Restored to its former glory after the 1994 Northridge earthquake, it's now a mainstay of the NoHo Arts District. Shows run on three stages (42 to 360 seats). (☎818-508-4200; www.elportaltheatre.com; 5269 Lankershim Blvd; 🚇Red Line to North Hollywood)

Baked Potato   JAZZ, BLUES

15 ⭐ Map p144, D5

Near Universal Studios, a dancing spud beckons you to come inside this diminutive jazz-and-blues hall where the schedule mixes no-names with big-timers. Drinks are stiff and actual baked potatoes ($6.50 to $15) are optional. (www.thebakedpotato.com; 3787 Cahuenga Blvd; cover $10-25, plus 2 drinks; ⏱7pm-2am)

Shopping

It's a Wrap!   CLOTHING

16 🔒 Map p144, F1

Here are fashionable, post-production wares worn by TV and film stars. What that means to you is great prices on mainstream designer labels, including racks of casual and formal gear worn on such shows as *Nurse Jackie* and *Scandal*. The suits are a steal and so is the denim. New arrivals are racked by show affiliation. (☎818-567-7366; www.itsawraphollywood.com; 3315 W Magnolia Blvd; ⏱11am-7pm Mon-Fri, to 6pm Sat, noon-6pm Sun)

Americana at Brand   MALL

17 🔒 Map p144, H3

If you dig the Grove (p66) in Mid-City then you'll enjoy this set-piece shopping mall, developed by the same folks, that feels like an extended walking street. There's an 18-screen multiplex, some 30 restaurants and food stalls and some very good, albeit very corporate, shopping. (www.americanaatbrand.com; 889 Americana Way, Glendale; ♿)

Top Sights
Disneyland & Disney California Adventure

Getting There

🚗 Anaheim is 25 miles southeast of Downtown LA on the I-5 Fwy.

🚆 Trains stop at **ARTIC** transit center. Then take a taxi or shuttle to Disneyland.

Mickey is one lucky mouse. Created by animator Walt Disney in 1928, this irrepressible rodent is a multimedia juggernaut, and he lives in Disneyland, the 'Happiest Place on Earth.' It's a slice of 'imagi-neered' hyper-reality, where the streets are always clean, the park employees – called cast members – are always upbeat, and there's a parade every day of the year. Even cynics must admit that since opening his home to guests in 1955, Micky's been a pretty thoughtful host to millions of blissed-out visitors.

Main Street USA

Fashioned after Walt's hometown of Marceline, Missouri, bustling Main Street USA resembles the classic turn-of-the-20th-century, all-American town. It's an idyllic, relentlessly upbeat representation, complete with barbershop quartet, penny arcades, ice-cream shops and a steam train.

Great Moments with Mr Lincoln, a 15-minute audio-animatronic presentation on Honest Abe, sits inside the fascinating **Disneyland Story** exhibit. Nearby, kids love seeing early Disney cartoons like *Steamboat Willie* inside **Main Street Cinema**.

Main Street ends in the **Central Plaza**. Lording over the plaza is **Sleeping Beauty Castle**, the castle featured on the Disney logo. Inside the iconic struc-ture (fashioned after a real 19th-century Bavarian castle), dolls and big books tell the story of Sleeping Beauty. As if you didn't know it already.

Tomorrowland

Even if 1950s imagineers envisioned the future as a galaxy-minded community filled with rockets and Googie-style architecture, these days, the *Star Wars* franchise gets top billing. **Hyperspace Mountain**, Tomorrowland's signature attraction and one of the USA's best roller coasters, hurtles you into complete darkness at frightening speed, and **Star Wars Launch Bay** shows movie props and memorabilia.

Meanwhile, **Star Tours** clamps you into a Starspeeder shuttle for a wild and bumpy 3-D ride through the desert canyons of Tatooine on a space mission.

If it's retro high-tech you're after, he **monorail** glides to a stop in Tomorrowland, its rubber tires traveling a 13-minute, 2.5-mile round-trip route to Downtown Disney. Just outside Tomorrowland station, kiddies will want to shoot laser beams on **Buzz Lightyear Astro Blaster** and drive their own miniature cars in the classic **Autopia** ride. Then jump aboard the **Finding Nemo Submarine Voyage** to look for the world's most famous clownfish from within a refurbished submarine and rumble through an underwater volcanic eruption.

Fantasyland

Fantasyland is filled with the characters of classic children's stories. One timeless attraction is '**it's a small world**,' a boat ride past hundreds of audio-animatronic children from a world of cultures all singing an ear-worm of a theme song.

Another classic, the **Matterhorn Bobsleds**, is a steel-frame roller coaster. Fans of old-school attractions will also get a kick out of *The Wind in the Willows*–inspired **Mr Toad's Wild Ride**, a loopy jaunt in an open-air jalopy through London.

Younger kids love whirling around the **Mad Tea Party** teacup ride and **King Arthur Carrousel**, then cavorting with characters in nearby **Mickey's Toontown**, a topsy-turvy minimetropolis where kiddos can traipse through Mickey and Minnie's houses and dozens of storefronts.

☑ 714-781-4636

www.disneyland.com

1313 Harbor Blvd

adult/child 3-9yr 1-day pass from $97/91, 2-day park-hopper pass $244/232

☑ Top Tips

▶ Disneyland Resort has three main areas: the theme parks Disneyland Park and Disney California Adventure, and Downtown Disney, an outdoor pedestrian mall.

▶ To **stay overnight** (☑ 800-225-2024, reservations 714-956-6425; www.disneyland.com), try the original Disneyland Hotel or the stunning Grand Californian Hotel.

▶ Disneyland Resort is open every day. During peak summer season, Disneyland's hours are usually 8am to midnight; the rest of the year, 10am to 8pm or 10pm. DCA closes at 10pm or 11pm in summer, earlier in the off season.

✕ Take a Break

There's no shortage of restaurants inside the resort.

Frontierland

This Disney 'land' is a salute to old Americana: the Mississippi-style paddle-wheel **Mark Twain Riverboat**, the 18th-century replica **Sailing Ship Columbia**, a rip-roarin' Old West town with a shooting gallery and the **Big Thunder Mountain Railroad**, a mining-themed roller coaster. The former Tom Sawyer Island – the only attraction in the park personally designed by Uncle Walt – has been reimagined in the wake of the *Pirates of the Caribbean* movies and renamed the **Pirate's Lair on Tom Sawyer Island**.

New Orleans Square

New Orleans Square has all the charm of the eponymous city's French Quarter but none of the marauding drunks. New Orleans was the favorite city of Walt and his wife Lillian, and he paid

---

Understand
FASTPASS & MaxPass

Lines for Disneyland Resort rides and attractions can be long, but the FAST-PASS and MaxPass system can significantly cut your wait times.

▶ Walk up to a FASTPASS ticket machine – located near attraction entrances – and insert your park entrance ticket or annual passport. You'll receive a slip of paper showing the 'return time' for boarding (it's always at least 40 minutes later).

▶ Show up within the window of time on the ticket and join the ride's FAST-PASS line. There'll still be a wait, but it's shorter (typically 15 minutes or less). Hang on to your FASTPASS ticket until you board the ride.

▶ If you're running late and miss the time window printed on your FASTPASS ticket, you can still try joining the FASTPASS line, although showing up before your FASTPASS time window is a no-no.

▶ What's the catch? When you get a FASTPASS, you will have to wait at least two hours before getting another one (check the 'next available' time printed at the bottom of your ticket).

▶ Before getting a FASTPASS, check the display above the machine, which will tell you what the 'return time' for boarding is. If it's much later in the day, or doesn't fit your schedule, a FASTPASS may not be worth it. Ditto if the ride's current wait time is just 15 to 30 minutes.

▶ MaxPass is basically the same as FASTPASS, but it operates from the Disneyland app and costs $10 per day. It includes unlimited downloads from Disney PhotoPass and allows you to make reservations from your smartphone.

tribute to it by building this stunning square lined with restaurants and attractions.

Pirates of the Caribbean is the longest ride in Disneyland (17 minutes) and provided 'inspiration' for the popular movies. You'll float through the subterranean haunts of tawdry pirates, where dead buccaneers perch atop their mounds of booty and Jack Sparrow pops up occasionally. Over at the **Haunted Mansion**, 999 'happy haunts' – spirits, goblins, shades and ghosts – appear and evanesce while you ride in a cocoon-like 'Doom Buggy' through web-covered graveyards of dancing skeletons.

Adventureland

Loosely deriving its jungle theme from Southeast Asia and Africa, Adventureland has a number of attractions, but the hands-down highlight is the safari-style **Indiana Jones Adventure**. Nearby, little ones love climbing the stairways of **Tarzan's Treehouse**. Cool down on the **Jungle Cruise**, viewing exotic audio-animatronic animals from rivers of South America, India, Africa and Southeast Asia. And the classic **Enchanted Tiki Room** features carvings of Hawaiian gods and goddesses and a show of singing, dancing audio-animatronic birds and flowers.

Disney California Adventure

Across the plaza from Disneyland's monument to make-believe is **Disney California Adventure** (DCA), an ode

> ### Understand
>
> ## Fireworks, Parades and Shows
>
> The fireworks spectacular above Disneyland's Sleeping Beauty Castle, **Remember – Dreams Come True**, happens nightly. In **Mickey's Soundsational Parade**, floats glide down Main Street USA with bands playing a variety of music from Latin to Bollywood, accompanying costumed characters.
>
> DCA's premier show is the 22-minute **World of Color**, a dazzling nighttime display of lasers, lights and animation projected over Paradise Bay. It's so popular, you should get a FastPass ticket.

to California's geography, history and culture – or at least a sanitized, G-rated version. DCA, which opened in 2001, covers more acres than Disneyland and feels less crowded; it also has more modern rides and attractions.

Hollywood Land

California's biggest factory of dreams is presented here in miniature, with soundstages, movable props, and – of course – a studio store. **Guardians of the Galaxy: Mission BREAKOUT!** is the newest thrill ride, a tower with drops of 130ft through the elevator shaft. The less adventurous can navigate a taxicab through 'Monstropolis' on the **Monsters, Inc: Mike & Sulley**

to the Rescue! ride, and there's a one-hour live stage version of *Frozen*, at the **Hyperion Theater**.

Grizzly Peak

Grizzly Peak is DCA's salute to California's natural and human achievements. Its main attraction, **Soarin' Around the World**, is a virtual hang-gliding ride using Omnimax technology that 'flies' you over famous landmarks. Enjoy the light breeze as you soar, keeping your nostrils open for aromas blowing in the wind.

Grizzly River Run takes you 'rafting' down a faux Sierra Nevada river – you will get wet, so come when it's warm. While fake flat-hatted park rangers look on, kids can tackle the **Redwood Creek Challenge Trail**, with its 'Big Sir' redwoods, wooden towers and lookouts, and rock slide and climbing traverses.

Cars Land

This land gets kudos for its incredibly detailed design based on the popular Disney Pixar *Cars* movies. Top billing goes to the wacky **Radiator Springs Racers**, a race-car ride that bumps and jumps around a track painstakingly decked out like the Great American West.

Tractor-towed trailers swing their way around the 'dance floor' at **Mater's Junkyard Jamboree**, or ride inside cars choreographed to classic retro tunes at **Luigi's Rollickin' Roadsters**. Route 66–themed gift shops and diners like the tipi-style Cozy Cone Motel will take on that special glow of nostalgia underneath neon lights in the evening.

Paradise Pier

If you like carnival rides, you'll love Paradise Pier at DCA, designed to look like a combination of all the beachside amusement piers in California. The state-of-the-art **California Screamin'** roller coaster resembles an old wooden coaster, but it's got a smooth-as-silk steel track: it feels like you're being shot out of a cannon. Just as popular is **Toy Story Midway Mania!** – a 4D ride where you earn points by shooting at targets while your carnival car swivels and careens through an oversized, old-fashioned game arcade.

Downtown Disney

Downtown Disney is a triumph of marketing. Once in this open-air pedestrian mall, sandwiched between the two parks and the hotels, it may be hard to extract yourself. There are plenty of opportunities to drop cash in stores (not just Disney stuff either), restaurants and entertainment venues. Apart from the Disney merch, a lot of it is shops you can find elsewhere, but in the moment it's still hard to resist. Most shops here open and close with the parks.

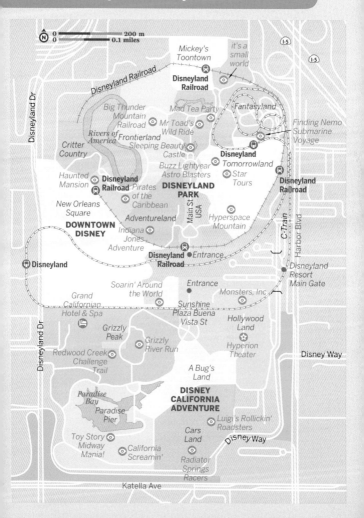

The Best of
Los Angeles

Los Angeles's Best Walks

Los Angeles's Best...

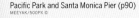

Pacific Park and Santa Monica Pier (p90)
MEEYAK/500PX ©

Best Walks
The Venice Stroll

🏃 The Walk

Step into the Venice lifestyle and rub shoulders with folks who believe that certain truths will only be revealed to those who disco-skate in a Speedo-and-turban ensemble. And, while such people may exist largely in their own universe, they happen to know that there are more moments of Zen packed into this tiny beach community than in most other 'hoods combined.

Start Ocean Front Walk and Washington Blvd; 🚌BBB 1

Finish Abbot Kinney Blvd; 🚌MTA 33

Length 3.5 miles; two hours

✕ Take a Break

The best place to put your feet up is one of the many cafes and restaurants along Abbot Kinney Blvd. If you're hungry for a quick bite, consider the takeout counter operated by **Gjelina** (p112).

Muscle Beach (p107)

❶ South Venice Beach

South of the Venice Pier is the untrammeled **beach** of South Venice.

❷ Venice Canals

Even many Angelenos have no idea that just a couple of blocks away from the boardwalk madness is an idyllic neighborhood that preserves 3 miles of **canals** (p109) of the late developer and tobacco mogul Abbot Kinney.

❸ Venice Boardwalk

The famed **Venice Boardwalk** (p106) is a vortex for the loony, the free-spirited, the hip and athletic. Here you'll find outdoor gyms, beach rentals, skate parks and drum circles.

❹ Muscle Beach

Gym rats with an exhibitionist streak can get a tan and a workout at this famous **outdoor gym** (p107) right on the Venice Boardwalk where Arnold once bulked up alfresco.

⑤ Venice Beach Art Walls

Keep your camera at the ready as you approach the tagged-up towers and freestanding concrete wall of **Venice Beach Art Walls** (p107), forever open to aerosol artists to curb vandalism.

⑥ Venice Skatepark

Long the destination of local skate punks, the concrete at **Venice Skatepark** (p107) has been molded and steel-fringed into 17,000 sq ft of vert, tranny and street terrain with unbroken ocean views.

⑦ Figtree's Cafe

If you're hungry already, **Figtree's Cafe** (www.figtreescafe.com; 429 Ocean Front Walk; appetizers $8-13, mains $11-16; ☺8am-9pm) serves the best eats on the Boardwalk.

⑧ Ballerina Clown & the Chiat/Day Buildings

On Main St are two of Venice's more captivating buildings. The **ballerina clown** rises like a twisted god/goddess from the corner of Main and Rose on an otherwise pedestrian building. Across the street is Gehry's epic **Chiat/Day** building.

⑨ Abbot Kinney Boulevard

Abbot Kinney, the man who dug the canals and christened the town, would probably be delighted to find the stretch of his namesake **boulevard** (p109) stacked with unique, individually owned boutiques, galleries and sensational restaurants.

Best Walks
The Downtown Hustle

The Walk

Downtown is the most historical, multi-layered and fascinating part of Los Angeles. There's great architecture, from 19th-century beaux arts to futuristic Frank Gehry. There's world-class music at the Walt Disney Concert Hall, top-notch art at the Museum of Contemporary Art (MOCA), superb dining and a Fashion District. You'll see it all as you explore this power nexus, creative vortex and ethnic mosaic.

Start LA Live; Ⓜ Pico

Finish Union Station; Ⓜ Union Station

Length 3.8 miles; three hours

Take a Break

When you're doing the downtown hustle, the **Grand Central Market** (p121) is a good reason to pause. Both for its byzantine wholesale market and recently updated food stalls.

KIT LEONG/SHUTTERSTOCK ©

Union Station (p128)

❶ The Grammy Museum

Music lovers will get lost in interactive exhibits that define, differentiate and link musical genres, while live footage strobes from all corners at the **Grammy Museum** (p126). Easily the highlight of LA Live.

❷ Fashion District

The axis of the **Fashion District**, this 90-block nirvana for shopaholics is the intersection of 9th and Los Angeles Sts, where fashionistas and designers congregate.

❸ Broadway Theater District

Highlighted by the still-running **Orpheum Theatre** (p123), built in 1926, and the recently redone **United Artists Theatre** (p134), **Broadway** was LA's entertainment hub with no fewer than a dozen theaters built in a riot of styles.

❹ Pershing Square

The hub of downtown's historic core, **Pershing Square** was LA's first public park, and is now enlivened by public art and summer concerts.

❺ Grand Central Market

The ground floor of the1905 Beaux-Arts **Grand Central Market** (p121) is where architect Frank Lloyd Wright once kept an office.

❻ Museum of Contemporary Art

The **MOCA Grand** (p126), housed in a building by Arata Isozaki, has a collection that arcs from the 1940s and includes works by Mark Rothko and Dan Flavin.

❼ Walt Disney Concert Hall

A molten blend of steel, music and psychedelic architecture, Gehry pulled out all the stops for the iconic **Walt Disney Concert Hall** (p120).

❽ Pueblo de Los Ángeles

Here's where LA's first colonists settled in 1781.

Pueblo de Los Ángeles (p128) preserves the city's oldest buildings.

❾ Union Station

A glamorous Mission Revival achievement with art deco accents, **Union Station** (p128) opened in 1939 as America's last grandrail station. Bukowski worked at the historic Terminal Annex post office just north of the station.

Best
Food

Bring an appetite. A big one. LA's cross-cultural make up is reflected at its table, which is an epic global feast. And while there's no shortage of just-like-the-motherland dishes – from Cantonese *xiao long bao* to Ligurian *farinata* – it's the takes on tradition that really thrill. Ever tried Korean-Mexican tacos? Or a vegan cream-cheese donut with jam, basil and balsamic reduction? LA may be many things, but a culinary bore isn't one of them.

The Big Shots

OK, so somewhere along the way chefs became celebrities, and the kitchen became a stage, and that arguably all started in Beverly Hills with Wolfgang Puck and Spago in the 1980s. It's also true that ever since then the world's best chefs have flocked to these celebrified streets to serve power lunches and dinners, and bask in the glow of Hollywood stars, and then partner with them. These days, chefs such as Nobu Matsuhisa, Thomas Keller, Mario Batali, Ludovic Lefebvre, Brooke Williamson, Jon Shook & Vinny Dotolo and Michael Voltaggio are among the culinary celebs ready to serve you.

Food Trucks

Any LA foodie will tell you that some of the best bites in town come on four wheels, with mobile kitchens serving up a global feast of old- and new-school flavors. Track food trucks at Roaming Hunger (www.roaminghunger.com), or check the websites, Twitter or Instagram feeds of favorites like Free Range (www.freerangela.com), Guerrilla Tacos (www.guerrillatacos.com), Kogi BBQ (http://kogibbq.com), Plant Food for People (http://pffp.org), Ta Bom Truck (www.tabomtruck.com) and Yeastie Boys (http://yeastieboysbagels.com).

☑ Top Tips

▶ Check out Pulitzer Prize winner Jonathan Gold's food column in the *LA Times*. He was the subject of Laura Gabbert's 2016 documentary feature *City of Gold*, a culinary love letter to LA.

▶ Many restaurants are open seven days a week, though some close Sunday and/or Monday.

Best in Town

Cassia Contemporary East-West fusion that hits the mark and smashes it. (p95)

Otium Nuanced modern-American flavors and clever cocktails. (p121)

Left: Eateries in Grand Central Market (p121); Above: Steak at Musso & Frank Grill (p32)

Gjelina Sharing plates packed with verve and knockout thin-crust pizza. (p112)

Petit Trois Ludo Lefebvre's tiny, no-reservations spot for Gallic-inspired fare. (p31)

Best Old-School LA

Canter's 24/7 Kosher classics, a giant bakery and hipster nightspot, the Kibitz Room. (p81)

Cole's A Downtown basement tavern famed for its French Dip sandwich and backroom speakeasy. (p130)

Musso & Frank Grill Direct from Hollywood's Golden Age. (p32)

Bob's Big Boy Googie diner within spitting distance of Warner Bros Studios. (p147)

Nate 'n Al Old-time, old-school Beverly Hills deli. (p62)

Casita del Campo Mexican flavors with a side of kitschy '60s decor and basement drag. (p49)

Best Standout LA Bites

Petit Trois Decadent Big Mec double cheeseburger. (p31)

Cassia Vietnamese pot-au-feu with short ribs, veggies and bone marrow at Cassia. (p95)

HomeState Soul-coaxing brisket sandwich. (p47)

MB Post Squid-ink tagliatelle with piquillo pepper, tomato ragu, Thai basil and breadcrumbs at MB Post. (p117)

Madcapra Soft, warm, made-from-scratch red falafel sandwich. (p130)

Crossroads Vegan artichoke 'oysters'. (p81)

Salt & Straw Almond brittle with salted ganache ice cream. (p110)

Sqirl Burnt brioche with house-made ricotta and jam. (p48)

Eggslut Fairfax sandwich. (p110)

Best
Drinking

Whether you're after an organic Kurimi espresso, a craft cocktail made with peanut-butter-washed Campari, or a saison brewed with Chinatown-sourced Oolong tea, LA pours on cue. From post-industrial coffee roasters and breweries to mid-century lounges, classic Hollywood martini bars and cocktail-pouring bowling alleys, LA serves its drinks with a generous splash of wow. So do the right thing and raise your glass to America's finest town.

Hot Trend: Cold Press

Southern California claims to have invented the fruit smoothie, but these days a much hotter recent trend is cold-pressed juice. While conventional juices are produced using fast-spinning blades to tear apart the produce, cold-pressed juices are made by pressing the liquid. The process reputedly protects the juice from heat and excessive oxidation, resulting in a drink with a greater concentration of vitamins, minerals and live enzymes.

Simple and Straight

Some of us prefer not to have complexities such as pomegranate or grapefruit juice; simple syrup and freshly snipped herbs get in the way of a fine spirit. Does this mean we lack taste? It simply suggests that when we go out drinking, we seek establishments that serve only the best rums, tequilas, mescals, whiskeys and bourbons distilled from this sweet earth, and when we finally arrive at the bar, we peruse the selection, order something generally high end, usually aged, and always neat.

☑ **Top Tips**

▶ Many bars in LA will require proof of age upon entry, no matter how old you look. Always take your driver's license or another form of official photo ID, or risk being refused entry.

▶ Under California law, the blood alcohol percentage limit is .08 percent. Don't even think about drinking and driving if you might be over that – it's both illegal and irresponsible. Cab or rideshare it.

▶ Downtown offers countless hip and tasty scenes within a short stroll.

Bar Marmont (p63)

Best Hard Stuff

El Carmen LA's ultimate tequila and mescal tavern has over 100 to choose from. (p82)

Harvard & Stone Craft whiskey, bourbon and daily cocktail specials. (p36)

Bar Marmont Sunset Strip classic that still delivers. (p63)

Varnish Cubby-hole-sized speakeasy, where good live jazz burns Sunday through Tuesday. (p133)

Best Cocktails with a View

Onyx Santa Monica's only indoor-outdoor roof bar has a swinging-'70s, Studio 54 vibe. (p99)

Upstairs at the Ace Hotel Knockout Downtown views, powerful cocktails and a luxe, safari-inspired fit-out. (p133)

Best Old School LA

Chez Jay Dark and dank beachside bar that's hosted the Rat Pack to the Brat Pack. (p98)

Frolic Room Hollywood's true dive, a vinyl-lined relic that has served them all, from Judy Garland to Charles Bukowski. (p25)

Polo Lounge Dress up and swill martinis in the Beverly Hills Hotel's legendary bar. (p64)

Dresden Legendary mid-century lounge famously shown in *Swingers*. (p49)

Best Beer

Mikkeller DTLA Slick design and cognoscenti brews conspire at Downtown's Danish import. (p133)

Library Alehouse Work your way through 29 microbrews in oceanside Santa Monica. (p98)

Best Dive Bars

Frolic Room A real-deal, anti-glam Hollywood dive frequented by the late Charles Bukowski. (p25)

New Jalisco Bar Cheap drinks and a thirst for fun lures hipsters and Latinos to Downtown's wild gay dive. (p132)

Best
Live Music

The history of music in LA might as well be the history of American music, at least for the last 75 years. Much of the recording industry is based here, and the film and TV industries have proven powerful talent incubators. The sheer abundance of world-class musicians, paired with spectacular and historic venues, makes it a minor tragedy to leave town without a concert in the memory files.

Night Music

Just like the perfect set of waves, or that first spring rain you can never be quite sure when, or if, it will happen. You do know that if your fellows are open of mind, and the musicians of the moment are generous of heart, there will be the possibility of greatness; of feeling new and alive in the Southern California night. Whether they be the hippie rockers and electronic mixologists of Echo Park, or the jazz cats of LACMA, whether they belong to the local philharmonic or are simply blasting through town and exploding on legendary stages like the global pop virtuosos they have become, there will be night music in Angel City. Download the Bandsintown smartphone app for daily listings.

Best Stages

Hollywood Bowl LA's greatest gift to musicians and their fans. (pictured above; p36)

Greek Theatre Almost as perfect as the Bowl. (p49)

El Rey A converted movie theater which hosts terrific indie acts. (p83)

Echo & Echoplex An edgy mix of DJ-driven dance parties and new rockers. (p53)

Fonda Theatre Hosts rising acts and residencies from legends. (p38)

Best Free Concert Venues

LACMA Friday means live jazz on the plaza for six months a year. (p75)

Grand Performances World music delights a packed plaza during the summer. (p134)

Getty Center Off the 405; events bring in alt rockers and world music. (p69)

Santa Monica Pier Thursday nights bring live music throughout the summer. (p100)

Best
Gay & Lesbian

LA is one of the country's gayest cities. Your gaydar may well be pinging throughout the county, but the rainbow flag flies especially proudly in Boystown, along Santa Monica Blvd in West Hollywood, flanked by dozens of high-energy bars, cafes, restaurants, gyms and clubs. Most cater to gay men but also welcome lesbians and mixed audiences. Other prominent LGBT districts include Silver Lake and Long Beach, and there's a growing Downtown scene.

GABRIEL OLSEN/CONTRIBUTOR/SHUTTERSTOCK ©

LGBT Festivals

West Hollywood's annual **Halloween Carnaval** (www.visitwesthollywood.com/halloween-carnaval) draws a crowd of 500,000 to Santa Monica Blvd. June's **LA Pride** (www.lapride.org) parade and festival is traditionally a celebration of diversity that brings huge crowds to the neighborhood with exhibits and shows – the 2017 version took on a different angle as an LGBT-rights protest march.

Best Nightspots

The Abbey It's been called the best gay bar in the world, and who are we to argue? (p63)

Akbar (☎323-665-6810; www.akbarsilverlake.com; 4356 W Sunset Blvd, Silver Lake; ⏰4pm-2am) Fun-loving, Casbah-style spot for queer Eastsiders of all ages.

Bar Mattachine Craft cocktails and a chill, friendly, modern vibe. (p132)

Eagle LA (☎323-669-9472; www.eaglela.com; 4219 Santa Monica Blvd, Silver Lake; ⏰4pm-2am Mon-Fri, from 2pm Sat & Sun; 📶) As close as LA gets to a proper gay leather bar.

Best Shows

Celebration Theatre (☎323-957-1884; www.celebrationtheatre.com; 6760 Lexington Ave, Hollywood) Ranks among the nation's leading stages for LGBT plays.

Cavern Club Theater Drag shows and other fabulously kooky performances beneath a Mexican restaurant. (p49)

Gay Men's Chorus of Los Angeles (www.gmcla.org) This amazing group has been doing it since 1979.

Best
Shopping

Consider yourself a disciplined shopper? Get back to us after your trip. LA is a pro at luring cards out of wallets. After all, how can you not bag that super-cute vintage-fabric frock? Or that tongue-in-cheek tote? And what about that mid-century-modern lamp that perfectly illuminates that rare, signed Hollywood film script? Creativity and whimsy drive this town, right down to its racks and shelves.

Keep it Indie, Keep it Local

Here's the one knock on the indie shops, labels and boutiques: they're all so damn expensive when compared to the Banana Republics of the world. But if you're into shopping with honor, and espouse a 'do no harm' lifestyle, then seek out LA's indie boutiques. You might make a sample sale in the Fashion District, and hunt down startup designers on the streets of the Arts District, Silver Lake, Echo Park and Venice. Little Tokyo also offers a scattering of idiosyncratic stores that are not just Japanese.

High End, Darling

Heavyweight fashion houses cluster around Melrose Pl; Fred Segal has two such outposts. Just know that if you do enter these hallowed halls, you will want to buy everything, compulsively seek out ever more obscene price tags in a blind 'but-I-want-these!' rage and you may whimper, even as you fork over a week's pay for a pair of stockings or some eyeliner. But, hey, this is LA, baby. There's no crying at the register!

Best Shopping Strips

Melrose Ave Everyone from the Olsen twins to the Kardashians have their boutiques. (p66)

Abbot Kinney Blvd Eclectic, artful mix of unique and indie boutiques by the beach. (p109)

Best Coastal Living

General Admission High-end beach towels, surf wear and gear. (p114)

Aviator Nation Feel good in signature hoodies and casuals. (p115)

Bo Bridges Gallery Beach-style art photography. (p117)

Left: Abbot Kinney Blvd (p109); Above: Book Soup (p66)

Best Offbeat

Spitfire Girl Our favorite gift shop in the city is a quirky cute staple. (p51)

Wacko A warehouse of kitsch, with a welcome literary impulse. (p51)

Mystic Journey New Age in Old Venice. (p114)

Best Pre-loved Finds

Luxe De Ville Impeccably maintained, runway-worthy. (p50)

It's a Wrap! Cast-offs from real TV shows and movies. (p149)

Amoeba Music Epic repository of vinyl, DVDs, CDs and collectables. (p39)

Best Books

Last Bookstore in Los Angeles An independent giant in a former Downtown bank. (p135)

Book Soup A legendary bookstore with author events in WeHo. (p66)

Skylight Books A snug, community-minded bookstore in Los Feliz, with obscure titles and regular events. (p51)

Mystery Pier Books Get your Christie fix in new and collectible editions in WeHo. (p66)

Worth a Trip

Everyone from today's hipsters to Hollywood costumers comes to shop at **Retro Row's** (www.4thstreetlongbeach.com; 4th St btwn Cherry Ave & Junipero St, Long Beach) vintage stores. If you only have time for one shop make it **Meow** (562-438-8990; www.meowvintage.com; 2210 E 4th St; noon-7pm Mon-Fri, 11am-7pm Sat, noon-6pm Sun). The owner has quite an eye, making it hard not to find something you didn't know you needed.

Best
For Kids

Los Angeles is sometimes touted as not especially child friendly, and looking around Rodeo Dr or the Sunset Strip, you might think that young Angelenos have been banished to a gingerbread cottage in the woods. In reality, LA offers a plethora of child-friendly attractions, from theme parks to interactive museums.

MAYK_SHALUNTS/SHUTTERSTOCK ©

Best Districts for Kids

At the beaches, parents can wear out their tykes with cycling and swimming, as well as in LA's parks, where hiking, exploring and animal watching are top notch.

Young *Animal Planet* devotees can ogle humanesque chimps at Griffith Park's LA Zoo (p46), while future paleontologists can study skeletal sabretoothed cats pulled from the La Brea Tar Pits (p72). The Petersen Automotive Museum (p78) has been recently refurbished with new kid-centric exhibits.

And, of course, don't forget the kiddiest destinations of all, theme parks, with options ranging from all-day happiness at Disneyland (p151) and Universal Studios (p142) to lower-key (and lowerbudget) thrills at Pacific Park (p91).

Best Animal Watching

Los Angeles Zoo 1100 finned, feathered and furry friends from over 250 species. (p46)

Best Outdoor Fun

Griffith Park One of the country's largest urban green spaces and one perfect carousel. (p46)

Echo Park Lake Take a pedal boat or a canoe out among the ducks, swans and the gushing fountain. (p53)

Manhattan Beach A gorgeous sweep of golden sand walking distance from an ice-cream parlor that might change your life. (p117)

Santa Monica Pier & Beach Kids love the venerable pier, where attractions include a quaint carousel, a solar-powered Ferris wheel and tiny aquarium with touch tanks. The beach ain't bad either. (p90)

Best Indoor Fun

Magicopolis Magic shows. 'Nuff said. (p100)

Best Kid-Friendly Museums

Griffith Observatory Grab a seat in the planetarium by day, peer into telescopes on the lawn by night. (p42)

California Science-Center The Space Shuttle, a simulated earthquake and a giant techno-doll named Tess bring out the kid in all of us. (p137)

Natural History Museum This museum will take you around the world and back millions of years in time. (pictured left; p137)

Best Kid-Friendly Restaurants

Bob's Big Boy Classic diner with kid-friendly menu. (p147)

Uncle Bill's Pancake House Grab an ocean-view table among the sexy surfers, tottering

toddlers and gabbing girlfriends. (p117)

Original Farmers Market A jumble of stalls and restaurants with something for even the most finicky eaters. (p82)

Best for Budding Artists

Getty Center Child-friendly interactive displays, a kids gift shop, entertainment and play-friendly gardens. (p69)

LACMA Giant sculptures and a hands-on children's gallery will keep little art fiends buzzing. (p74)

Worth a Trip

In Long Beach, on LA's southern border with Orange County, the **Aquarium of the Pacific** (tickets 562-590-3100; www.aquariumofpacific.org; 100 Aquarium Way, Long Beach; adult/senior/child $30/27/19; 9am-6pm;) is a vast, high-tech indoor ocean where sharks dart, jellyfish dance and sea lions frolic. More than 11,000 creatures inhabit four re-created habitats: the bays and lagoons of Baja California, the frigid northern Pacific, tropical coral reefs and local kelp forests. Across the harbor, the legendary ocean liner **Queen Mary** (877-342-0738; www.queenmary.com; 1126 Queens Hwy, Long Beach; tours adult/child from $27/17.50; tours 10am-6pm or later; ; Passport, AquaBus, AquaLink) is permanently moored; you can enjoy the hokey but fun Ghost & Legends Tour.

Best
Outdoor
Adventure

KRIS DAVIDSON/LONELY PLANET ©

Despite spending a lot of time jammed on freeways, Angelenos love to get physical. Theirs is a city made for pace-quickening thrills, with spectacular mountain hikes, one of the country's largest urban nature reserves and surf-pounded beach, making it a mecca for fitness buffs since early days. Residents hike, beach and work out at the gym with almost religious fervor. With almost 300 days of sunshine you'll forgive the locals for looking so, so good.

Hiking

If hiking doesn't feel like an indigenous LA activity to you, you need to reassess. This town is hemmed in and defined by two mountain ranges and countless canyons. **Modern Hiker** (http://modernhiker.com) is a virtual encyclopedia of hiking trails around LA.

Beach Volleyball

Beach volleyball originated in Santa Monica during the 1920s and has become an Olympic sport. You'll find nets set up up and down LA County's beaches, especially in Santa Monica, Venice and Manhattan Beach, where **AVP (Association of Volleyball Professionals) Pro Beach Volleyball tournaments** (www.avp.com; Manhattan Beach; ⏰mid-Aug) happen every summer.

Extreme Sports

Extreme sports in SoCal go back to the 1970s when skateboarders on the Santa Monica–Venice border honed their craft by breaking into dry swimming pools in the backyards of mansions (the 2005 film *Lords of Dogtown* chronicles their rise).

Best Beaches

Venice Boardwalk
Mecca for surfers, cyclists, skaters and 'bladers. (p106)

Santa Monica Beach
Best choice for families, with the famous pier close by for entertainment. (pictured above; p91)

Manhattan Beach Lots of space, lots of waves, lots of class. (p117)

Best Short Hikes with Views

Hollyridge Trail Part of **Griffith Park** but best accessed from Bronson Canyon, this trail leads to just below the Hollywood Sign. (p46)

Runyon Canyon It's a hike, it's a workout, it's a pick-up spot with a view. (p30)

Best
Beaches

With miles and miles of wide, sandy beaches, you'll find it hard to resist getting wet in LA. Beach life and surf culture are part of the free-wheeling SoCal lifestyle, so play hooky any day of the week and go hit the waves like locals so often do.

What to Wear

Beachwear is appropriate along the coastal strip, but not in the rest of LA. 'No shoes, no shirt, no service' signs appear in establishments all over town.

Surf's up! You down?

Even if you've never set foot on a board, surfing tints every aspect of LA beach life, from clothing to lingo. The most powerful swells arrive in late fall and winter, while May and June are generally the flattest months, although they do bring warmer water. Speaking of temperature, don't believe all those images of hot blonds surfing in skimpy swimsuits – without a wet suit, you'll likely freeze your butt off except at the height of summer. Outfitters in Santa Monica and elsewhere can provide gear and lessons.

Best People-Watching

Venice Boardwalk Let your freak flag fly! (p106)

Santa Monica State Beach Best choice for families, with the famous pier close by for entertainment. (p91)

MARKUS KULLAMA/SHUTTERSTOCK ©

☑ Top Tips

▶ California's ocean currents bring water down from Alaska, meaning it's chilly much of the year. Ocean temperatures for swimming become tolerable by about May, peaking in July and August.

Manhattan Beach Lots of space, lots of waves, lots of class. (p117)

Best for Beachcombing

El Matador Rocky spires in the swirling tides. (pictured above; p103)

Best Celebrity-Spotting

Admit it. You want to see a celeb. Of course you do. You're in Hollywood. So don't apologize for it. Maybe it's the talent we love, or feeling connected to the world through one anointed person, or thinking we'll absorb a bit of the holy glow. Or maybe they're just hot and cool, or...hot.

CHARLEY GALLAY/STRINGER/GETTY IMAGES ©

Getting Your Star Fix

According to a University of Southern California study, actors tend to be more narcissistic than the rest of society. Uh, yeah, and too much cheese is fattening.

That said, it suggests that fan-love sates their needs as well as your own. So, how to fulfill two needs with one gawk? Driving past stars' homes is a start, but it's unlikely you'll see anyone. As for velvet rope clubs, you very well may not get in.

So where to look for stars? In their natural habitat, of course. Restaurants are primo, especially in Hollywood, West Hollywood and Mid-City. As for cinemas, spotting celebs at the ArcLight Hollywood (p37) is a good bet.

Shopping works too, so browse their faves on Robertson Blvd and Abbot Kinney Blvd. Finally, hillside trails are favored for exercise. Who *was* that jogging past in the baseball cap?

Popular Celeb-Spotting Spots

Fred Segal Top-shelf shopping yields top-shelf shoppers. (p84)

Barneys New York Celebs often shop here and dine at the deli. (pictured above; p67)

Celebrity Spotting Almost Guaranteed

Bar Marmont Weeknights only. (p63)

Nobu Malibu A handy go-to for oceanside stars. (p103)

Runyon Canyon Don't let those baseball caps

☑ Top Tips

▶ You're pretty much guaranteed to see stars at a live TV-show taping.

▶ About the only stars you're likely see on Hollywood Boulevard are the brass and marble ones in the sidewalk.

and shades fool you. Even the stars love hiking the hills. (p30)

Melrose Ave Paparazzi, skinny jeans, heels and scented candles. (p66)

Grove Everyone from Justin Bieber to Demi Lovato and Kylie Jenner shops at this polished outdoor mall. (p66)

Warner Bros Studio Tour They work here, don't they? (p146)

Best
Museums

Museums grand and austere, sprawling and magical, tucked away and hidden in plain sight, dot Greater Los Angeles. If you're not feeling culturally aware, awake or relevant in LA, you won't be alone, but it will be your own fault.

ANTON_IVANOV/SHUTTERSTOCK ©

Best Museums

Getty Center Stunning location, groundbreaking architecture, rotating exhibits and timeless treasures. (pictured above; p69)

Broad World-class contemporary art collection in a dynamic new building. (p126)

LACMA LA's top art museum, stocked with fine art and global antiquities. (p74)

Hammer Minor works by Monet, Van Gogh and Mary Cassatt, and cutting-edge contemporary exhibits. (p58)

Petersen Automotive Museum Futuristic salute to *vroom vroom*, in the city that defined car culture. (p78)

Grammy Museum Come here and trace the history of American popular music. (p126)

Hollywood Museum If granny's attic were crammed with movie and TV costumes and props... (p25)

Best Alternative Realities

Museum of Jurassic Technology Be warned, there is madness lurking in this rabbit hole. (p87)

Wall Project A fat slab of the fallen Berlin Wall blessed with work from street artists, via the Wende Museum. (p79)

☑ **Top Tips**

▶ Some of LA's best museums are open free to the public, including the Broad, Getty and Hammer. Others offer specific free days or at least a few hours free a week. Check websites for details.

▶ The Anne Frank Exhibit at the Museum of Tolerance is sensational.

▶ It's worth paying the extra buckage to tour the Petersen Automotive Museum's vault.

Best
Tours

Whether you're interested in the seeds of LA noir, ghost hunting, ethnic nibbling, soaking in neon, architecture, art, or peering at the many sides of the Angel City from a road bike, we've got you covered.

Get Deep, Get Weird, Get Real

Whatever your pleasure – dark or light, tragic or profane, sweet and tasty – there is a tour for you. There exists a tour of scandal and blood, you may gawk at the stars (and their dirt) with actual paparazzi, tour a working studio in Burbank or Hollywood, or gaze at world-class architecture downtown.

History & Architecture

Los Angeles Conservancy (☏213-623-2489; www.laconservancy.org; adult/child $15/10) Weekend walking tours exploring LA's architectural treasures.

Esotouric (☏213-915-8687; www.esotouric.com; tours $58) Offbeat tours of LA's intriguing, sometimes gruesome underbelly.

Film & TV Studios

Warner Bros Studio Tour Snoop around where movie magic is made. (p146)

Paramount Pictures The only studio still in Hollywood proper. (p28)

Art & Culture

Out & About Tours (www.thelavendereffect.org/tours; tours from $30) Walking tours of LA's LGBT history.

Neon Cruise (☏818-696-2149; www.neonmona.org; tours $55; ⏱usually 7-10:30pm Sat, twice monthly Jun-Sep) Offered by the Museum of Neon Art.

INGUS KRUKLITIS/SHUTTERSTOCK ©

TMZ Celebrity Tour Tour Hollywood hangouts with celebrity-spotting specialists. (p28)

Outdoor Adventure

Bikes & Hikes LA (☏323-796-8555; www.bikesandhikesla.com; 8250 Santa Monica Blvd, West Hollywood; self-guided/guided tours from $39/52, bike rentals per hour/day from $8.50/32) A 32-mile 'LA in a Day' bike tour to kick your butt while you sightsee.

Food & Drink

Melting Pot Food Tours (☏424-247-9666; www.meltingpottours.com; adult/child from $59/45) Come hungry to hit the culinary hotspots of Mid-City, Pasadena and more.

Survival Guide

Survival Guide

Before You Go

When to Go

Los Angeles

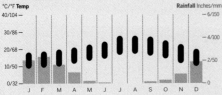

°C/°F **Temp**
40/104 —
30/86 —
20/68 —
10/50 —
0/32 —

Rainfall Inches/mm
— 6/150
— 4/100
— 2/50
— 0

J F M A M J J A S O N D

➡ **Winter** (December to February) Wettest season, particularly January and February, though there's still plenty of sunshine, with average highs of around 68°F (20°C) in the Downtown area. Good hotel deals, though demand is high in February due to the Academy Awards.

➡ **Spring** (March to May) Ideal time to visit. Average rainfall drops dramatically by April and the oppressive summer heat and crowds of summer are still at bay. Decent hotel deals are still available.

➡ **Autumn** (September to November) Another favorable period. Summer crowds have thinned, though temperatures remain warm. Average rainfall remains low, especially in September. Nights can be chilly toward November.

Book Your Stay

LA is huge. Do your research before booking a room or house. Do you want to be within stumbling distance of hot-spot bars and clubs, near major cultural sites, or by the ocean? Unless you plan on driving (and spending time in traffic), find a place close to major metro or bus routes.

Most neighborhoods have hotels in just about every price range. Expect to pay between $150 and $300 per night for a midrange room.

Useful Websites

Lonely Planet (www.lonelyplanet.com/usa/los-angeles) Destination information, hotel bookings, traveler forum and more.

Discover Los Angeles (www.discoverlosangeles.com) Official Convention and Visitors' Bureau website.

A Curbed (www.
a.curbed.com) Delicious
sites of history, neighborhood esoterica and celeb-
rity real-estate gossip.

Eater LA (http://la.eater.
com) Up-to-the-minute
news and reviews cover-
ing the city's ever-evolving food scene.

LA Times (www.latimes.
com) Excellent coverage
of local news, arts and
culture.

Los Angeles Magazine
(www.lamag.com) Up-
to-date news and articles
covering LA dining, arts,
fashion, civic issues and
more. Also offers handy
Things to Do' lists.

Best Budget

**HI Los Angeles-Santa
Monica** (www.hilosangeles.
org) Budget-friendly digs
that rival facilities at
properties costing many
times more.

USA Hostels Hollywood
(www.usahostels.com) Af-
fordable budget digs with a
busy social calendar in
Hollywood.

Best Midrange

Mama Shelter (www.
mamashelter.com) A cheeky,
smart-casual hangout in
hip-again Hollywood.

Line Hotel (www.thelineho
tel.com) A cool, minimalist
hotel in the heart of food-
obsessed Koreatown.

Best Top End

Montage (www.montage
beverlyhills.com) A sceney
rooftop pool and five-star
spa steps from Rodeo Dr.

Malibu Beach Inn (www.
malibubeachinn.com)
Coveted art, ocean views
and interiors that make
interior designers rave.

Shutters on the Beach
(www.shuttersonthebeach.
com) A New England–
style retreat in Santa
Monica.

Dream (www.dreamhotels.
com) Hollywood's latest
designer slumber hot
spot.

Arriving in Los Angeles

Los Angeles International Airport

LAX (LAX; www.lawa.org/
welcomeLAX.aspx; 1 World
Way) is the main LA gate-
way, with nine terminals

including **Tom Bradley
International Terminal**,
hub for most interna-
tional air carriers.

➡ Terminals are linked by
the free **LAX Shuttle A**,
leaving from the lower
(arrival) level of each
terminal. **Cabs** and hotel
and car-rental **shuttles**
stop here as well.

➡ **LAX FlyAway** (☎866-
435-9529; www.lawa.org/
FlyAway) runs to Union
Station (Downtown LA),
Hollywood, Van Nuys
(San Fernando Valley),
Westwood Village (near
UCLA) and Long Beach.
A one-way ticket costs
$9.75.

➡ The **Disneyland Resort
Express** (☎800-828-6699;
www.graylineanaheim.com;
⏱7:50am-8pm) travels
hourly or half-hourly from
LAX to the main Disney-
land resorts (adult/child
one way $30/22, round
trip $48/36).

➡ For scheduled bus
services, catch the free
shuttle bus from the
airport toward parking
lot C. It stops by the LAX
City Bus Center hub for
buses serving all of LA
County. For Santa Monica
or Venice, change to the
**Santa Monica Big Blue
Bus** lines 3 or Rapid 3
($1.25). If you're headed

for Culver City, catch **Culver City Bus** 6 ($1). For Manhattan, Hermosa or Redondo Beaches, hop aboard **Beach Cities Transit** 109 ($1).

➜ LAX rail service is currently under construction. For now, take a free LAX shuttle to lot G and board the **Metro Green Line** light rail. For Downtown LA, change at Willowbrook/Rosa Parks station to the Metro Blue Line light rail toward 7th St/Metro Center. The rail journey to Downtown takes about one hour.

Burbank Hollywood Airport

Some domestic flights operated by Alaska, American Eagle, Delta Connection, JetBlue, Southwest and United also arrive at **this airport** (BUR, Bob Hope Airport; www. burbankairport.com; 2627 N Hollywood Way, Burbank), convenient to Hollywood, Downtown or Pasadena.

Long Beach Airport

Near LA County's southern border, with Orange County, the small **Long Beach Airport** (www.lgb. org; 4100 Donald Douglas Dr, Long Beach) is convenient for Disneyland and is

served by Alaska, JetBlue and Southwest.

Union Station

Interstate trains on **Amtrak** (www.amtrak. com) trains roll into Downtown's historic **Union Station** (☏800-872-7245; www.amtrak.com; 800 N Alameda St).

Greyhound Bus

The main bus terminal for **Greyhound** (☏213-629-8401; www.greyhound. com; 1716 E 7th St) is in an industrial part of Downtown, so try not to arrive after dark.

Getting Around

Public Transport

Most public transportation is handled by **Metro** (☏323-466-3876; www. metro.net), which offers maps, schedules and trip-planning help through its website.

To ride Metro trains and buses, buy a reusable TAP card. Available from TAP vending machines at Metro stations with a

$1 surcharge, the cards allow you to add preset cash value or day passes. The regular base fare is $1.75 per boarding, or $7 for a day pass with unlimited rides. Both single-trip tickets and TAP cards loaded with a day pass are available on Metro buses (ensure you have the exact change). When using a TAP card, tap the card against the sensor at station entrances and aboard buses.

TAP cards are accepted on DASH and municipal bus services and can be reloaded at vending machines or online on the TAP website (www.taptogo.net).

Metro Rail

The Metro Rail network consists of two subway lines, four light-rail lines and two express bus lines. Six lines converge in Downtown LA. The most useful lines for visitors are:

Red Line The most useful for visitors. A subway linking Downtown's Union Station to North Hollywood (San Fernando Valley) via central Hollywood and Universal City.

Expo Line Light-rail line linking Downtown with

Exposition Park, Culver City and Santa Monica. It connects with the Red Line at 7th St/Metro Center station.

Gold Line Light-rail line running from East LA to Little Tokyo/Arts District, Chinatown and Pasadena via Union Station.

7th St/Metro Center station is the main transfer point for the Red and Expo (as well as Blue and Purple) lines.

Most lines run from around 4:30am to 1am Sunday to Thursday, and until around 2:30am on Friday and Saturday nights. Frequency ranges from up to every five minutes in rush hour to every 10 to 20 minutes at other times.

Metro Buses

Metro operates about 200 bus lines across the city and offers three types of bus services:

➜ Metro Local buses (painted orange) make frequent stops along major thoroughfares throughout the city.

➜ Metro Rapid buses (painted red) stop less frequently and have special sensors that keep traffic lights green when a bus approaches.

➜ Commuter-oriented Metro Express buses (painted blue) connect communities with Downtown LA and other business districts and usually travel via the city's freeways.

Municipal Buses

Santa Monica–based **Big Blue Bus** (☎310-541-5444; www.bigbluebus.com) serves much of western LA, including Santa Monica, Venice, Westwood and LAX ($1.25). Its express bus 10 runs from Santa Monica to Downtown ($2.50, one hour).

The **Culver City Bus** (www.culvercity.org/enjoy/culver-city-bus) runs services throughout Culver City and the Westside. This includes a service to Aviation/LAX station on the metro Green Line ($1), from where a free shuttle connects to LAX.

Long Beach Transit (www.lbtransit.com; $1.25 per ride) serves Long Beach and surrounding communities. ($1.25 per ride.)

All three municipal bus companies accept payment by TAP card.

DASH Buses

These small, clean-fuel shuttle buses, run by the LA Department of Transportation (www.ladottransit.com), operate along 33 routes serving local communities (50¢ per boarding, 0.25¢ for seniors and passengers with disabilities), but only until around 6:30pm to 7pm and with limited services on weekends. Many lines connect with other DASH routes; see the website for details. Here are some of the most useful lines:

Beachwood Canyon Route (Monday to Saturday) Useful for close-ups of the Hollywood sign; runs from Hollywood Blvd and Vine St up Beachwood Dr.

Downtown Routes (daily) Five separate routes hit all the hot spots. Route A runs from Little Tokyo to City West, Route B connects Chinatown to the Financial District, Route D travels between Union Station and South Park, Route E connects City West to the Fashion District, and Route F connects the Financial District to Exposition Park and USC. Routes A, B and D do not run on weekends.

Fairfax Route (Monday to Saturday) Makes a handy loop past the

Beverly Center mall, the Pacific Design Center, western Melrose Ave, the Farmers Market/Grove and Museum Row.

Hollywood Route (daily) Covers Hollywood east of Highland Ave and links with the short Los Feliz Route (daily) at Franklin Ave and Vermont Ave.

Car & Motorcycle

Unless time is no factor – or money is extremely tight – you're going to want to spend some time behind the wheel, although this means contending with some of the worst traffic in the country. Avoid rush hour (7am to 9am and 3:30pm to 6pm).

Parking at motels and cheaper hotels is usually free, while fancier ones charge anywhere from $8 to around $45 for the privilege. Valet parking at nicer restaurants and hotels is commonplace, with rates ranging from $3.50 to $10.

The usual international car-rental agencies have branches at LAX and throughout LA, and there are also a couple of companies renting hybrid vehicles. If you don't have

a vehicle already booked, use the courtesy phones in the arrival areas at LAX. Offices and lots are outside the airport, but each company has free shuttles leaving from the lower level.

For Harley rentals, go to **Route 66** (📞888-434-4473, 310-578-0112; www.route66riders.com; 4161 Lincoln Blvd, Marina Del Rey; 🕐10am-6pm Mon-Sat). Rates start from $149 per six hours, or $185 for one day. Discounts are available for longer rentals.

Taxi

➡ Because of LA's size and its traffic, getting around by cab will cost you.

➡ Cabs are best organized over the phone, though some prowl the streets late at night, and they are always lined up at airports, train stations, bus stations and major hotels.

➡ Fares are metered and vary by the company. The **Uber**, **UberX** and **Lyft** smartphone apps are extremely popular for cheaper rides in LA.

➡ In the city of LA, taxi rates are $2.85 at flagfall plus about $2.70 per

mile. Cabs leaving from LAX charge a $4 airport fee. For details, check www.taxicabsla.org. Taxi companies include the following:

Beverly Hills Cab (📞800-273-6611; www.beverlyhillscabco.com) A solid, dependable company, with good rates to the airport and a wide service area.

Checker (📞800-300-5007; http://ineedtaxi.com) Services both the airport and a large swathe of the LA metro area.

Taxi Taxi (📞310-444-4444; www.santamonicataxi.com) Easily the best and most professional fleet available. It'll drive you anywhere, but can only pick up in Santa Monica.

Essential Information

Business Hours

➡ Normal business hours are 9am to 5pm Monday to Friday. Banks usually open from 8:30am to 4:30pm Monday to

hursday and to 5:30pm
n Friday; some also
pen from 9am to 2pm
n Saturday.

• Shops open from 10am
o 7pm Monday to Sat-
rday, though shopping
nalls may close later, and
pen from 11am to 6pm
n Sunday.

• Bars are generally open
rom late afternoon until
am.

• Restaurants generally
erve lunch from 11am
o 3pm and dinner from
:30pm to 10pm.

Electricity

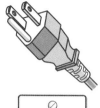

Type B
120V/60Hz

Type A
120V/60Hz

Emergency

**Ambulance, fire &
police** ☎911

Public Holidays

On the following national
holidays, banks, schools
and government offices
(including post offices)
close, and transporta-
tion, museums and other
services operate on a
Sunday schedule. Holi-
days falling on a weekend
are usually observed the
following Monday.

New Year's Day
January 1

**Martin Luther King Jr
Day** Third Monday in
January

Presidents' Day Third
Monday in February

Good Friday Friday
before Easter (March/
April)

Memorial Day Last
Monday in May

Independence Day
July 4

Labor Day First Monday
in September

Columbus Day Second
Monday in October

Veterans Day
November 11

Thanksgiving Day
Fourth Thursday in
November

Christmas Day
December 25

Safe Travel

Despite its seem-
ingly apocalyptic list of
dangers – guns, violent
crime, earthquakes – Los
Angeles is a reasonably
safe place to visit. The
greatest danger is posed
by car accidents (buckle
up – it's the law), while
the biggest annoyance is
city traffic.

Earthquakes happen
all the time, but most are
so tiny they are detecta-
ble only by sensitive seis-
mological instruments. If

you're caught in a serious shaker:

➡ If indoors, get under a sturdy desk or table and cover your head and neck with your arms. If in bed in the dark, stay in bed and cover your head and neck with a pillow.

➡ Stay clear of windows, mirrors or anything that might fall.

➡ Don't head for elevators or go running into the street.

➡ If you're in a shopping mall or large public building, expect the alarm and/or sprinkler systems to come on.

➡ If outdoors, get away from buildings, trees and power lines.

➡ If you're driving, pull over to the side of the road away from bridges, overpasses and power lines.

➡ Stay inside the car until the shaking stops.

➡ If you're on a sidewalk near buildings, duck into a doorway to protect yourself from falling bricks, glass and debris.

➡ Prepare for aftershocks. Turn on the radio and listen for bulletins. Use the telephone only if absolutely necessary.

Telephone

Foreign GSM multiband phones will work in the USA. Popping in a US prepaid rechargeable SIM card is usually cheaper than using your own network; they're sold at any major telecommunications or electronics store.

City Codes

US phone numbers consist of a three-digit area code followed by a seven-digit local number. In Greater Los Angeles, dial 1 before all digits.

Select area codes around Los Angeles:

Anaheim ☎ 657, 714

Beverly Hills, Culver City, Malibu, Santa Monica, South Bay ☎ 310, 424

Burbank, San Fernando Valley ☎ 747, 818

Echo Park & Downtown LA ☎ 213

Hollywood, Los Feliz, Mid-City, Silver Lake ☎ 323

Pasadena & San Gabriel Valley ☎ 626

Useful Phone Numbers

Country code ☎ 1

International dialing code ☎ 011

Operator ☎ 0

Directory assistance ☎ 411

Tipping

Hotel bellhops $2 per bag, or minimum $5 per cart.

Concierges No tips required for simple information; up to $20 for securing last-minute restaurant reservations, sold-out show tickets etc.

Housekeeping staff $2 to $5 daily.

Room service 18% to 20%, unless a gratuity is already charged.

Parking valets At least $2 when handed back your car keys.

Tourist Information

Los Angeles Visitor Information Center (☎ 323-467-6412; www.discoverlosangeles.com; Hollywood & Highland, 6801 Hollywood Blvd; ⏰ 8am-10pm Mon-Sat, 9am-7pm Sun; Ⓜ Red Line to Hollywood/Highland) The main tourist office for Los Angeles, located in Hollywood. Maps, brochures and lodging information, plus ickets to theme parks and attractions.

Beverly Hills Visitors Center (☎ 310-248-1015; www.lovebeverlyhills.com; 9400 S Santa Monica Blvd, Beverly Hills; ⏱ 9am-5pm Mon-Fri, from 10am Sat & Sun; 🔊) Sightseeing, activities, dining and accommodation information focused on the Beverly Hills area.

Downtown LA Visitor Center (www.discover losangeles.com; Union Station, 800 N Alameda St; ⏱ 9am-5pm; Ⓜ Red/Purple/Gold Lines to Union Station) Maps and general tourist information in the lobby of Union Station.

Visit Pasadena (☎ 626-795-9311; www.visitpasadena.com; 300 E Green St, Pasadena; ⏱ 8am-5pm Mon-Fri, 10am-4pm Sat) Visitor information with a focus on Pasadena attractions and events.

Santa Monica Visitor Information Center (☎ 800-544-5319; www.santamonica.com; 2427 Main St) The main tourist information center in Santa Monica, with free guides, maps and helpful staff.

Visit West Hollywood (www.visitwesthollywood.com; Pacific Design Center Blue Bldg, 8687 Melrose Ave, Suite M60, West Hollywood; ⏱ 9am-5pm Mon-Fri; 🔊) Information on attractions, accommodation, tours and more in the West Hollywood area.

Travelers with Disabilities

➡ Telephone companies provide relay operators (dial 711) for the hearing impaired.

➡ Many banks provide ATM instructions in braille.

➡ Download Lonely Planet's free Accessible Travel guide from http://lptravel.to/Accessible-Travel.

➡ **A Wheelchair Rider's Guide to the California Coast** (www.wheeling calscoast.org) is a free online directory and downloadable PDF guide for LA and Orange County coasts covering wheelchair access at beaches, parks and more.

➡ **Los Angeles for Disabled Visitors** (www.discoverlosangeles.com) offers tips for accessible sightseeing, entertainment, museums and transportation.

➡ **Society for Accessible Travel & Hospitality** (TTY; ☎ 212-447-7284; www.sath.org)

Behind the Scenes

Send Us Your Feedback

We love to hear from travelers – your comments help make our books better. We read every word, and we guarantee that your feedback goes straight to the authors. Visit **lonelyplanet.com/contact** to submit your updates and suggestions.

Note: We may edit, reproduce and incorporate your comments in Lonely Planet products such as guidebooks, websites and digital products, so let us know if you don't want your comments reproduced or your name acknowledged. For a copy of our privacy policy visit lonelyplanet.com/privacy.

Acknowledgements

Climate map data adapted from Peel MC, Finlayson BL & McMahon TA (2007) 'Updated World Map of the Köppen-Geiger Climate Classification', Hydrology and Earth System Sciences, 11,1633–44.

Cover photograph: Venice Beach, Wendy Connett/Alamy ©

Contents photograph: Sunset at Venice Beach, Giorgio Fochesato/Getty Images ©

This Book

This 5th edition of Lonely Planet's *Pocket Los Angeles* guidebook was curated by Andrew Bender, who also researched and wrote it along with Cristian Bonetto. The previous two editions were written by Adam Skolnick. This guidebook was produced by the following:

Destination Editor Clifton Wilkinson **Product Editor** Kathryn Rowan **Senior Cartographer** Alison Lyall **Book Designer** Mazzy Prinsep **Assisting Editors** Andrew Bain, Maja Vatrić **Cartographer** Julie Dodkins **Cover Researcher** Marika Mercer **Thanks to** Imogen Bannister, Michelle Coxall, Shona Gray, Karin Hartman, Sarah Stocking, Tony Wheeler

Index

See also separate subindexes for:

⊗ **Eating** p189

☺ **Drinking** p190

☺ **Entertainment** p190

🔒 **Shopping** p191

A

Abbot Kinney Boulevard 109
accommodations 178-9
Ace Gallery 78
Annenberg Community Beach House 94
Aquarium of the Pacific 171
area codes 184
Arts District 87
Autry Museum of the American West 46

B

Barnsdall Art Park 46
beaches 173
Beverly Hills, see West Hollywood & Beverly Hills
bicycling 112
Bikes & Hikes LA 59
Binoculars Building 110
Blum & Poe 87
Bo Bridges Gallery 117
Broad 126
Bronson Canyon 46
Burbank & Universal City 140-9, **144-5**
drinking 148-9
entertainment 149

Sights 000
Map Pages **000**

food 146-8
itineraries 141
shopping 149
sights 142-3, 146
transport 141
bus travel 181-2
business hours 182-3

C

California African American Museum 137
California Heritage Museum 94
California Science Center 137
Capitol Records Tower 29
car travel 182
Carousel 94
C.A.V.E. 110
CBS Television City 78
celebrity chefs 60
celebrity-spotting 174
cell phones 16
children, traveling with 170-1
City Hall 126-7
climate 178
comedy clubs 65
costs 16
Craft & Folk Art Museum 78
Culver City 86-7, **86**
currency 16
cycling 112

D

disabilities, travelers with 185
Disney California Adventure 150-5
Disneyland 150-5
Dodger Stadium 53
Dolby Theatre 25
Downtown 118-35, **124-5**
drinking 132-3
entertainment 134
food 129-32
itineraries 119, 122-3, **122**
shopping 134-5
sights 120-1, 126-9
transport 119
walks 160-1, **161**
Downtown Art Walks 123
drinking 164-5

E

Echo Park 52-3, **52**
Echo Park Lake 53
Edgemar 94-5
Egyptian Theatre 30
El Capitan Theatre 30
El Matador State Beach 103
El Pueblo de Los Ángeles Historical Monument 128
electricity 16, 183

emergencies 183
Exposition Park 136-7

F

Fashion District 122-3
Fashion Institute of Design and Merchandising 122
food 162-3
Forest Lawn Memorial Park - Hollywood Hills 146
Frederick R Weisman Art Foundation 59-60

G

Gamble House 139
gay travelers 63, 132, 167
Getty Center 68-9
Getty Villa 103
Gold Bug 139
Gold's Gym 109
Grammy Museum 126
Grauman's Chinese Theatre 25
Greystone Mansion & Park 60
Griffith Observatory 42-3
Griffith Park 46
Griffith Park, Silver Lake & Los Feliz 40-51, **44-5**
drinking 49
entertainment 49-50

Our Writers

Andrew Bender

Andrew is a native New Englander who worked in the financial industry in Tokyo and the film industry in Los Angeles before setting out to pursue his dream of traveling and writing about it. He has since authored more than three dozen LP titles as varied as *Japan, Korea, Taiwan, Norway, Amsterdam, Germany* and to his current home of *Southern California*. He also writes the Seat 1A travel site for Forbes.com, and contributes to the *Los Angeles Times* and airline magazines. Catch his work at www.wheres-andy-now.com.

Cristian Bonetto

Cristian has contributed to over 30 Lonely Planet guides to date, including *New York City, Italy, Venice & the Veneto, Naples & the Amalfi Coast, Denmark, Copenhagen, Sweden* and *Singapore*. Lonely Planet work aside, his musings on travel, food, culture and design appear in numerous publications around the world, including *The Telegraph* (UK) and *Corriere del Mezzogiorno* (Italy). When not on the road, you'll find the reformed playwright and TV scriptwriter slurping espresso in his beloved hometown, Melbourne. Instagram: rexcat75.

Published by Lonely Planet Global Limited
CRN 554153
5th edition – Dec 2017
ISBN 978 1 78657 244 8
© Lonely Planet 2017   Photographs © as indicated 2017
10 9 8 7 6 5 4 3 2 1
Printed in Singapore